SPEAKING UNDER PRESSURE

PRESSURE

Learn From The Testimony and
Real-Life Experiences of
An Actor   A Spy   A Private Eye

Dennis Sakamoto
408-472-0893
dennis@thespeakershrink.com

SPEAKING UNDER PRESSURE

First published in 2017 by Amazon KDP in the United States

ISBN: 978-0-692-98243-3

Library of Congress Cataloging-in-Publication Data
Sakamoto, Dennis
  Speaking Under Pressure: Learn from the Testimony and Real-Life
  experiences of an Actor A Spy A Private Eye / Dennis Sakamoto

Control Number 2017917684
ISBN: 978-0-692-98243-3 (Cloth/Soft cover)
1. Public speaking 2. Business communication
3. Personal growth 4. Christian testimony

Cover Design by Mike Tanamachi
Book production by Shawn Morningstar

First Edition: December 2017

10 9 8 7 6 5 4 3 2 1

Printed in the United States

FOR ANDREA

Meet me at the Merry-Go-Round

Table of Contents

Act I:
SETTING THE STAGE
DEALING WITH THE REALITY OF PRESSURE

The Road To Hell Is Paved With Good Intentions
OR
Proverbs 14:12 *There is a way that seems to be right but in the end it leads to Hell.* (NIV)

Act II:
Here's How it's Really Done
SPEAKING UNDER PRESSURE

Ephesians 4:29 *Do not let any unwholesome talk come out of your mouths, but only what is helpful for building others up according to their needs, that it may benefit those who listen.* (NIV)

CHANGING YOUR INSIDE

CHANGING YOUR OUTSIDE

CHANGING YOUR FOCUS

Act III:

The Narrow Road to Joy Is Deeply Paved with Pain

COLOSSIANS 4:6 *Let your speech be always with Grace, seasoned with salt, that you may know how you ought to answer each one.*

Introduction

When I coach speaking, my specialty is to help the speaker make a real and significant change during one private session of less than two hours. This is intimate, intense, and with a complete stranger face-to-face. We cannot address everything, but we can find "the key" that is holding that person back from being the very best they can be.

I learned this from the culmination of my life's journey, as told by the real-life experiences in this book. If you look at what I have done, you can sum it up as a study in people.

There are no techniques or theories in this book. Every solution given to you has been done by me and witnessed in others, hundreds of times. Everything is proven and everything works.

About the Author

DENNIS SAKAMOTO

Private Investigator California License QM7692.

Counter-Intelligence Agent, 115th Military Intelligence Group

Sergeant, U.S. Army term of service 5 Dec 68 to 7 Sep 71

The Speaker Shrink (private coaching for speaking with executives, business speakers, key note address, authors going on tour, interviewing, TV panel, etc.)

Actor for twenty-one years (made my living in New York City and Los Angeles—forty-five TV commercials, movies, television, stage, voice, print modeling)

On-camera acting coach for thirty-four years (about three thousand students)

Producer, Director, Writer, independent movies and many videos

Producing Director Theatre (46 plays)

Bartender in the original wild disco days of New York City

Instructor of defensive firearms safety (helping others to not light themselves up)

P.S. If you do not think that the following will work for you, you got more than your money's worth out of me. You now know what the real problem is that is holding you back.

Dealing with the Reality of Pressure

The Road To Hell Is Paved With Good Intentions

OR

PROVERBS 14:12 *There is a way that seems to be right but in the end it leads to Hell.* (**NIV**)

The Missing Zen Statue—A True Tale

It was hot and still like a thousand other days in Los Angeles. I peeked out the dusty window screen, looking west at the brown air, searching hopelessly for rain clouds that never came.

My patient stake-out of the cheap ticking clock finally paid dividends. The hands pointed to 5:00pm. I could now crack open a long awaited first quart of beer, without being an alcoholic. The two chilled quarts stood tall on the refrigerator top shelf next to some crunchy looking catsup and an out of date mustard. Should I begin with the right jug or the left one? In life, important decisions need to be made. The right quart won out, after all, I was only drinking the second quart. The first quart of beer only counted for "cutting the dust."

My crummy portable TV sat dying on a crummier portable TV cart. The kind you can only purchase in garage sales. I flicked on the tube hoping that no one had messed with the rabbit ear antennas balanced on top of the ancient TV.

The disasters of the L.A. five o'clock news would easily justify the second quart of beer. I liked quarts of beer. They are a relic from the past. Doing things that no one else does anymore has always had a great appeal to me.

How was I to know that a future of trouble was fading in with the off color picture on screen. LIVE AT FIVE ACTION NEWS was reporting from the East Central Police Station. The East Central Police communication tower to be exact. High in the sky.

TV News cameras were recording live action. A desperate woman had climbed the high tower and was clinging for life at the top of the tower. All TV channels were well represented with reporters and camera crews. Frantic chaos circled the base of the high tower, as the woman spider screamed threats of jumping to her death below. I found it interesting that she spoke clearly and without any obscenities, as any good public speaker should, especially before this unruly business group and television audience.

There were two types of faces in the crowd below. One type was the familiar frantic media. The other type looked like they had been elected to clean the latrine. This second type was the police. They had not a hard-boiled look. They had not a "Protect and Serve" look. It was more of a look like sucking on a rotten lemon. They looked plenty fed up.

Soon the media spin became a dramatic comparison of the woman above to a poor lost kitten stuck high in a tree. Questions were broadcast, "Why are the police not doing anything?"

The Detectives must have drawn straws for who would make the first climb.

Something better be done for the LIVE AT FIVE audience. A younger flat stomached detective must have drawn the short straw. Our hero handed his jacket to a senior detective, with not so flat a stomach and some kind of odd smirk on his face. The senior detective cautioned the younger stud to leave his holstered sidearm behind. Rather than cheering the hero detective on, the still air seemed to be filled with deep sympathy from the other police.

Cheers broke out as the reluctant hero climbed onward and upward up the tall tower.

The woman, way up high, shifted her positioning and increased the volume of her threats to jump. She spoke loud and clear, with good presentation skills for a key note speech, to her audience who were, in this case, below.

Slowly but surely the detective took step by step up the tower. A fine mixture of the Los Angeles Police Department's Code "To Protect and To Serve" and thoughts of a family waiting back at home holding their wind.

Then, without warning, the woman above removed something from her rear pants pocket. She raised her hand and opened fire by pelting the detective below with small rocks. Rock pollution scattered the news crew below. LIVE AT FIVE has no such code of "To Protect and To Serve".

Our brave reluctant detective got really busy, holding on for dear life with one hand and fending off a shower of rocks with the other.

The news media was surprised. The police were not.

There are only so many falling rocks that one can absorb in the line of duty. The climbing detective found it best to retreat south. Round one went to the desperate woman in the sky, now raising her "power to the people" fist. This stand off would last a few hours, until either she needed more rocks or a restroom.

As I reached for the second quart of beer, I wondered who would climb a police communications tower to commit suicide, with a pocket full of rocks?

This Private Eye would have that answer in just 14 more sleeps.

Two Weeks Later

It was again hot, still, and brown in L.A. I didn't know whether I was in West Hollywood or West L.A. It didn't matter much as who ever heard of a Zen monastery in either? I parked my trusty egg-beater car on a street lined with houses out of the silent movie era; except now they all sported iron bars over the windows.

It wasn't my idea of a Zen monastery. It wasn't on top of a mountain. It was an old structure converted to a kind of Hollywood Zen clubhouse. I guess doorbells have no use in Zen, so I had to knock on the door. I would have much preferred a gong. Then I heard bare footsteps scrambling down the hall. They were heading toward me and I thought I heard something like, "Oh boy. Here we go!"

The huge door cracked open. I didn't see a monk or a vampire. A middle-aged man with the face of a business executive board member peeked out at me. He politely inquired, "Are you the private investigator?"

"Yes." I spoke under pressure, without giving too much away.

The door opened wider, revealing a string of middle-aged white people. I smelled Malibu Beach. No one wore robes. No monks. Just a row of t-shirts with some Zen wisdom displayed across everyone's chest. It took all I had to hide my deep disillusionment with a cute smile.

I glanced down at the shoes resting on the dark wood floor. Everyone wore expensive footwear. When the wealthy disguise themselves with a vow of poverty, they have a hard time parting with expensive quality shoes. Sometimes, you can tell a lot about people from their footwear. The Zen Chief Executive Officer (ZCEO) spoke as if I was about to be laid off, "Come in please," said the spider to the fly.

As I fell into the clubhouse, I could not help but notice the Zen Beverly Hills décor. Maybe the interior decorator wore a black robe. Incense smoke was thick in my honor. I held my tongue about how the smell of incense somehow makes me irritable.

Once inside, I was introduced to the chorus line. I didn't mind the bowing, but the serene tone of voices started to make me sleepy. I heard bare feet shuffling in another room. The ZCEO. filled me in, "The Roshi is being notified of your arrival. In the meantime, I will provide you with the details."

I coughed up a "Thank you." Again, this is called economy of speaking under pressure. Sometimes the most spiritual thing to do is to shut up.

He continued with pride, "Our monastery here was bestowed a great honor. A priceless gift of a hand carved Zen statuette. It was carved from rare sandalwood."

A picture was placed before me. Kind of an upscale wanted poster. The small sandalwood statue was a work of art. The ZCEO grimaced, "It was stolen last week. And we know who took it."

As if on cue, the Roshi made a serene floating entrance. He was Asian, had a shaved head, and wore a black robe. Now we're talking. That was good enough for me. I didn't know whether to stand or to bow. So I played it safe and didn't do either. The Roshi nodded to me and joined us on the overstuffed chairs and couches. He was a tiny man and well cast as a Zen monk. After slipping off his sandals, he pulled both feet way up on the seat. I wished that I could do that.

I was introduced formally, "This man is the Private Investigator we would like to hire to retrieve our statue."

The Roshi nodded his head with deep resign and settled his eyes down at the floor. I would have wondered if I had the measles, if it were not for recognizing this very Asian thing to do. Call it Buddhist resignation of my karma.

The ZCEO laid it on me, "The two young people who stole our priceless treasure are named Moira and T.J." I nodded my head. T.J.s always did it.

He shed a ray of sunlight, "Moira was recently on the TV news. She climbed a police tower."

"In East Central L.A." I added, smelling the Karma.

The sunlight glowed brighter, "You saw that! Wonderful!"

Sometimes a "Gulp" comes from the throat. Today, mine came from my tummy. I covered my "Gulp" with,

"Yeah, I watched that on LIVE AT FIVE. Is she Jewish?"

The ZCEO's eyelids jerked, "I really don't know. Why?"

"She's got chutzpah."

There was a quiet reflection, followed by a deep study into my scrutable face. A Japanese-American private eye speaking Hebrew. I sliced into the silence,

"What can I do for you?"

The leader seemed rehearsed, "We want you to find Moira and T.J.—that is all. We should then be able to retrieve our statue. We prefer to keep this to ourselves. It is our responsibility."

Knowing these two rustlers shouldn't be too hard to find, I assured all,

"I'll hunt them down."

The gulp now came from everyone else's tummy. The Zen executive jumped,

"No, No! Our way is not violence."

They must be from Malibu Beach. I restored the peace.

"No violence. And no police." As I flashed back on the disgusted look of the police at the tower, I assured them, "No cops. No media. Just us."

Business leadership began thinking bottom line. "Pardon me. How much is your fee?"

"$50 a day—plus expenses. It sounds like I won't need much ammo."

"Will there be anything else you may require?"

"I don't do divorces."

We shook hands closing his loop.

I got the rest of the primary poop from an excited group of white tanned Zen disciples. Everyone wanted to spill the beans. I learned...

Moira and T.J. have lived at the Zen monastery twice in the past few years. I didn't need to listen to how troubled the young couple was. They would show up all messed up. The kindly Zen followers practiced the way of compassion. Kind of like some Zen rehab. So the mission began helping these two lost souls.

Round one of Zen rehab did not go as planned. After sleeping a lot, eating even more, and doing a lousy job of mopping the floor, the two lost souls got their breath back and fled into the night for another boxing round with the world. If there were any missing items of fencing value, it did not matter. Moira and T.J. were chalked up to karma.

About a year ago, round two of rehab began with the return of the prodigal mess. This time they were really, really off their rockers. The two made amends for their former caper and swore vows of commitment culminating in shaving their heads, denouncing the world, and fasting from all cheeseburgers and fries. They seemed to have found their way.

When the Monastery was entrusted with the statue, the couple marveled at its spiritual beauty. Life was good. Too good…too fast.

For anyone addicted to alcohol, drugs, or crime, there is nothing more hazardous in the depths of rehab as life becoming too good.

Moira and T.J., true to habits, split the scene. They jumped on their motorcycle and rode off happily into the sunset. This time, nothing much was stolen, so memories of them remained warm and fuzzy.

A few weeks ago, the priceless Zen statue left the monastery on a motorcycle; last seen riding off into the sunset with a giggling Moira and T.J.

I checked out the application papers required of the couple for entrance into the monastery. The handwriting was so jumpy it might have a heart attack at any moment. Armed with promising phony addresses and references, I said Shalom to the hopeful group. Actually, I had acquired an honest taste in getting these good people back their priceless statue.

At this time in ancient history, there was no internet. So "leads" still had to be run down by feet and by wit. This hunt was made much simpler by looking for two people who were well known in their community. The two were equally hated by the police and by everyone else who had come into contact with them. Moira and T.J. walked with a dead or alive price on their heads. Mostly dead.

At their local courthouse, both were out on bail. Even in the court parking lot, their car was smashed up by lengths of pipe. I would guess that the devoted couple took this all in stride. Just par for the course. The gravity for Moira's arrest for climbing the police tower took a very distant place in respect to many other previous charges. And there was one charge that shined above all the rest.

Coaxing people to speak freely to you is an acquired skill (covered in this very book). Coaxing neighbors to speak freely about their neighbor that they hate takes far less coaxing. I found the secret to the missing Zen statue in such a neighborhood; as follows: Once upon a time, it started out as another quiet morning in a tired run down neighborhood of East Los Angeles. The time was likely around the percolating of the first coffee of the day.

Like every other boring morning, Moira stumbled out of her rented lopsided cottage and dragged her fractured slippers down the driveway; there was a clear path as her car was parked in the rear carport.

Down about the end of her driveway, Moira halted then swiveled her head in three different directions (criminals look around before making a move). She then pinched the front of her bathrobe and jammies together and bent over a bit towards her side. A newspaper was removed from her neighbor's driveway.

This quiet act of theft brought immediate consequences. Moira's neighbor burst out of his house screaming war cries into the still morning air. This fearless senior citizen charged the thief in a deadly challenge of torn bathrobes. Pent up resentments and accusations exploded in the morning air. Moira's neighbor made it clear that his morning newspaper would no longer be delivered to her.

Moira apologized, "I'll make things right. Wait here. Don't move."

The senior citizen needed to catch his breath, as Moira returned to the door of her lopsided cottage.

In the time that it takes to say your name, Moira came back out from her door and walked briskly toward her now silent neighbor. Her eyes locked in focus. She carried her neighbor's morning newspaper in her left hand and her right hand was plugged into her bathrobe pocket. An odd smile twisting her face began to unnerve her indignant neighbor.

Without so much as a breath (when taking care of business confrontation, if your opponent gets really-really quiet then uncross your legs and watch out), Moira raised out of her bathrobe pocket a Colt Government 45 Automatic pistol.

The 45 Automatic has been a preferred tool for social encounters since it's debut in 1911. However, this favored gun is not easy to master. Whenever possible, even experts use both hands while firing. This big pistol holds seven large 45 slugs in the magazine and one in the chamber.

With one hand filled with 45 and the other hand filled with the morning news, Moira opened up the ball and began target practice on her senior citizen neighbor.

There is nothing that will clear out a crowd of nosy neighbors faster than hosing down the neighborhood with 45 slugs. An orchestration of booms and screams played out a symphony of ear splitting chaos.

Sometimes we never really know the former life of beauty of an aged person. In this case, Moira's neighbor must have been a suave dancer in his day. Other neighbors and their grandchildren will for generations sing praises of his jitterbug moves on his lawn to the tune of a swinging 45.

In the definitive silence that follows eight gunshots, that old unscathed hoofer dashed back into his household, needing a change of location followed by a change of underwear.

Moira could only stare at her now empty smoking gun and dismal failure with deep dejection. Always have a backup when heading into social encounters. Her head rose as the sounds of approaching sirens drew close.

Nothing causes you to become an attention magnet for badges more than gunfire. It will even attract the police ninjas in black, known as SWAT.

The once quiet neighborhood, soon to be with dropping market values, was cordoned off. Moira's lopsided cottage was surrounded. Once again, LIVE AT FIVE reporters and crews stormed the location shoot. This saddened the police, removing the attractive option of burning the house down.

After a few hours of stand off, news media short attention span began to fester. Disappointed that Moira would have to be wanted alive, the decision was made to use gas. Tear gas is acceptable public relations for the TV audience. Others who had a history with the fugitive, must have been scratching their trigger fingers.

Tear gas is relatively harmless. In army basic training, we had to enter a tear gas chamber and then remove our gas masks surrounded by the thick smoke. We then got to put a hand on another's shoulder and move in a circle while singing three verses of, "The old gray mare ain't what she used to be." After our rendition, we were allowed to exit the gas chamber while in a coughing fit. The only significant consequence was since we all had the flu—the toes of all of our boots were covered with fallen snot. No better way is there to clear a stuffy nose than with tear gas.

Tear gas canisters crashed through the glass windows of the lopsided cottage. Smoke began to billow out of the jagged glass holes. The police took aim and prayed for their wishes. Hopefully, Moira would bust out blasting away.

In business or in relationships, it is not good to depend on expectations. They can lead to disappointments. Such as after the tear gas cloud fades away. Even police have children to pick up from day care. Like all business supervisors, even captains have to worry about the bottom-line and overtime. There comes a time when decisions need to be made against the clock.

The siege of the lopsided cottage was now in it's sixth hour. The news had to order reloads for their cameras. The time for hostile takeover had arrived.

An army of police ninjas in black stormed the fortress. Remember the Alamo! All was over in a heartbeat.

No one was in there. No gun. No snot. No Moira.

It is times like these when one does not wish to lead a company. What thought leader wants to try to answer the nagging question of "What now?"

A frantic search with blue and tan uniforms uncovered nothing. "What now" transitioned into "Now what?" The news media had a field day.

At seven hours into the stand off and search, a young rookie took it upon herself to think "outside the box" and look under Moira's car parked quietly in the rear carport. As the rookie peeked under the car, she came face–to-face with the escaped fugitive. Her innovation disrupted, Moira gave up without incident, either ready to surrender or ready to use the bathroom. She was hiding under her car the entire siege. Chutzpah.

It is amazing what you can accomplish in your business with enough chutzpah and the ability to keep your head under fire, surrounded by a bunch of people with gas.

Meanwhile, back to the Zen monastery. In mouth dropping silence and awe, the Malibu Beach disciples listened to my caper. Moira was up for big time attempted murder of her dancing neighbor. Shaving her head and hiding out in the monastery would not clear the smoke this round. She was facing years in prison. So it figures that climbing the police tower and stealing the priceless statue would work up a legal argument for being nutty as a fruitcake. With her colorful past, there would be plenty of witnesses to put nutty frosting on the cake.

After I had spilled the story about Moira creating eight 45 caliber holes in the air, I could feel tummies gurgling and courage running down legs.

I can't say that I blame them for altering any Zen views on death. After all, nobody wants to get lead poisoning. So my private eye karma was no longer required, as of immediately. I, of course, would be compensated plus expenses for a few quarts. I assured the followers that they would get their priceless statue back, as it would only do Moira good in court if it was returned unharmed.

I only hope that their hand carved Zen statue still remains priceless to them. The clock struck five. It must be time to cut the dust.

LESSON LEARNED

The behavior of people will tell you their character. Their character can predict their behavior. If they are selfish and self-centered, they will be very predictable. This will determine their perspectives of how they look at you and themselves, which will cause their actions taken upon you.

It's 3am in Greenwich Village

On the west side of lower Manhattan, erupts the famous and notorious neighborhood of Greenwich Village, known to New Yorkers as "The Village." Perhaps, because no one with a Brooklyn accent knows how to pronounce "Gren-ich".

Our United States was founded on revolution and rebellion. The Village followed likewise. From starving artists drinking their dinners to local printed handouts stir-frying war against the evil Wall Street, lying just to the east, The Village of the 1950's spawned "Beatniks" daring to grow facial hair and penning unintelligible verses of poetry, approved by the snapping of fingers. Coffee shops hosted penniless artsy readings not non-fat lattes.

I acted in forty-nine seat black box theatres in the depth of The Village. This was an alternative theatre known as Off-Off-Broadway. In these unconventional hole-in-the-wall boxes, you will not find revivals of huge musicals. You would more likely discover experimental plays with no commercial value, giving the Broadway Wednesday matinee theatre parties (known to the actors as: "The blue rinse crowd") a severe case of cardiac arrest.

Like all original artist's hide-outs, when fame comes to the area, the artists get the boot and the money moves in. But 1980 was still the twilight of nostalgia in The Village. There was still a remainder of the wild west of "Dodge City" on the streets. It was still a famous magnet for "wackos" and rebellion.

New York City was not a big city to many long time residents of neighborhood apartment living. I knew an elderly Jewish lady and also an Italian grandmother who rarely ventured beyond a three block radius of their rent controlled apartments. For them, the big city was a small town. Local blocks were defended with the pride and unity of a small country.

Once upon a time, I was acting in a movie. We were shooting on a hot humid summer night (not good weather for human behavior). We were scheduled for two location all night shoots near the rowdiest square in the bowels of The Village.

Accomplishing anything in New York City requires three times more money than anywhere else. The movie company must pay for a squad of police officers to maintain or establish order on the location. The costly fees for filming permits will cover the location but will never cover the people who rule the location.

Another movie, filming uptown in the Bronx, had to pay off blackmail to young entrepreneurs who caused trouble, making disruptive noise and actually poking the movie horses with the tips of their knives. All kinds of folks are attracted to the big budget of a major movie shoot

We were shooting action scenes on these two hot humid summer nights. In one sequence of shots, I was to kidnap the female lead star. She was directed to jump out of our moving car, with me then bailing out and chasing her. In the heat of the chase, the leading lady would turn and beat on me (the tough guy) with her purse. To finish off this silver screen encounter, the male lead star would ride up on his big motorcycle and pulverize me with his thick motorcycle anti-theft steel chain. The two stars would then escape, leaving yours truly in the gutter with the doggie residue where villains, like me, belong.

When you shoot on location, you film all day until the sun goes down or you film all night until the sun comes up. I showed up on location in The Village in the late afternoon for the night shoot's call time.

As I approached the huge white movie trucks parked neatly behind the police gated barricade, I saw the director rushing up towards me in a very pleased state. He had two huge anti-theft motorcycle chains, one in each hand. From his manner of approach, I thought he was reminding me that it might be my birthday. He halted in front of me and did his best to regain his English composure.

"So good to see you. Props has created this delightful stunt double chain!"

(Are you seeing where this is leading?) I stared at the two mean looking giant chains. He broke the silence of my study,

"The brilliant scene where you get slapped with the chain."

My delightful British director held up both chains. His smile flashed a slight gap in his front teeth,

"Your stunt double chain is made of al-you-min-ee-um."

As I do not speak British, I had to inquire,

"What is al-you-min-ee-um?"

More enthusiasm and more gap, "Al-you-min-ee-um! Al-you-min-ee-um!!!"

I jerked, "Do you mean a-loom-in-um?"

"Yes! Quite! Al-you-min-ee-um."

I took the two chains. After hefting both of them,

"Which one is the al-you-min-ee-um?"

Like a true film Director, he studied my eyes for truth, then a rather loud –

"Ha ha! Very good."

It must have been my emotional content that caused him to reassure,

"Stunts has a wet suit that you shall wear under your shirt."

"Cheers" I croaked.

The busy director turned to leave and I managed not to tell him to keep a stiff upper lip. I still could not guess which chain was which.

Darkness had crashed on The Village streets and my kidnapping scene with the leading lady was now recorded in movie history. All went well except for her height. She was about a head taller than I; so I had to devise a special wrist-lock to use on her as a come-along, or it might look like she captured me. I managed to force her into the car to end the shot.

The civilian on-looker crowd was growing in size. The high apartments around us had residents hanging out of the windows shouting a wide assortment of comments.

It was now show time for filming the moving car stunt. In desperate escape, the tall leading lady would jump out of our villain's car and I would then bail out in hot pursuit, in glory of the bad guy hall of fame.

For those of you who drive, if a car is in front of you and driving "only fifteen miles per hour," it seems very slow moving. However, if you open the car door and look down at the street moving inches below, "only fifteen miles per hour" seems very, very fast.

Because of the stunt, we would run only one camera rehearsal before going for the take. This would lead to the first disaster of the evening.

"Rehearsing!" was called through the bullhorn, followed by "Action!"

The leading lady jumped out of the moving car and I bailed out after her. We were running directly toward camera. The director and full crew stood behind the 35mm Panavision movie camera.

Now she claims to be five feet eleven inches tall but I say she is more like six feet two inches high. Being a star, she was also exercising and in great shape. At this time of my life, the main exercise I trained in was bending my elbow.

> **NOTE** Villains who chase tall women track stars should not drink alcohol.

In hot foot pursuit, I never even got close to her. After she left me in the village dust, she stood by the camera with a puzzled look on her face. She was barely winded and was staring at me with her hands on her hips.

I was literally hanging on to a street light post so as not to fall down in public. The movie crew, crowd of lookers, and neighborhood residents hanging out of their windows, were all roaring with laughter. It was like a comical version of being thrown to the lions in the Roman Colosseum. The English director turned to the leading lady beside him and as if ordering a cup of tea said,

"You are no longer running track at Yale."

Villains who can't catch the heroine are doomed to another take.

Take 2. "Action!" We jumped out of the moving car again, but this time I caught up to her (after she let me). I grabbed her arm and she spun around to smack me with her swinging purse. Now for the second disaster of my evening. After she smacked me a good one with the prop purse, I felt something warm running down my face. She stopped and her eyes squinted at my face. Not written in the script, she yelled,

"Medic! We have an injury!"

The buckle on the prop purse had not been secured properly so when it hit me, I got sliced above the right eye. Also not in the script was real blood trickling down my villain face. The Village Colosseum roared with blood thirsty approval.

Various movie crew rushed toward me. Rather than my welfare, I was reminded not to get my blood on my wardrobe.

The clock and darkness was ticking away during the expensive break in the filming. So rather than my going to emergency at Bellevue hospital, they closed me up with a styptic pencil, like I was some kind of boxer in the ring.

We managed to get the shot on the next take and needed to move on. I provided great entertainment value for the crowd and only wish I would have run a popcorn concession. Because of the blood, I was requested for autographs.

Next in the sequence of filming was a shot of the male lead star riding up on his big motorcycle to rescue the leading lady star from the beaten up yours truly. He would halt his motorcycle beside what was left of me and then polish me off with the mean looking al-you-min-ee-um prop chain. (now do you seeing where this is going?) I guess it was just my night for autographs.

The upper wet suit was fit under my shirt. This brilliant idea would serve to pad me from the impact of the chain hitting me. The glamour of Hollywood was beginning to wear off the crowd as it was getting to be 3am. Some real "nasties" were being screamed at us from above.

So we blocked the shot (movement rehearsal) under the street lights. I was instructed to turn and the leading man was to plaster me with the swinging chain. Because the neighborhood was becoming very unruly, we were to film the rehearsal, hoping to get the shot. Over the bullhorn –

"We are rolling! And Action!"

I timed the turn well and faced the upcoming leading man swinging the huge chain at my upper torso, which was supposed to be well protected with the hidden wet suit.

(What follows is why I do not believe in fancy theories to be used in the heat of human passion. This is where I would use the term habitual behavior, reacting out of fear and pressure during the process of conducting business).

As I turned, the huge chain swung at me and I, without thought or hesitation, did what is normal for me. I ducked! Because the chain was aimed at my upper torso, after I ducked, it of course hit me and wrapped around my neck. You can enjoy the same shot in some violent cartoons. Now it was the leading man's turn to register shock in his face. I was enjoying a one-hundred percent evening, I actually began to feel sorry for him.

The stunt coordinator rushed to me and tried to cover himself in business,

"Why did you duck?"

I did not dignify that with a reply.

After they unraveled me from the chain necklace, we set up right away for another take. I could feel the pressure rising everywhere.

"Camera's rolling! And action!"

You must understand that the leading man is a really nice guy. We got to know each other a bit in the early morning make-up room at the studio. We used to swap previous night adventures and escapes. It was he who later looked at my cut from the purse and assured me'

"Yup. That will scar."

After he saw my "Thanks buddy" expression, he promised me,

"Don't worry. Women love scars."

He then let me inspect his small hook shaped scar.

Meanwhile, back to the whip. The leading man drove the big motorcycle up to me and I turned. As he lifted the chain to hit me, I could see it in his eyes. Hesitation. He was a nice guy. His moment of hesitation caused the weight of the big motorcycle to shift under him and he almost was dumped over.

The potential for injuring the star during the shooting really got the director concerned. He asked the two of us to practice and get more comfortable. The crew was given a break. Still surrounded by a large crowd of onlookers, under the illumination of a street light, the leading man practiced hitting me with the prop chain. He would swing and hit me on the wet suit,

"Did that hurt?"

I assured him, "No, fine."

Another swing of the chain thudded against my back, he checked again,

"How was that?"

"You can go harder."

Then another harder swing of the chain,

"How was that for you?"

From the nearby crowd, the scream of a banshee roared in the night. A small male, with a trimmed goatee beard, burst through the crowd of onlookers. He sported black leather skin-tight pants, black leather tight vest open revealing his skinny pale chest, and a black motorcycle leather cap tipped rakishly on his head. He jumped over the police barricade and charged the two of us. He screamed at the leading man,

"Hit me! Hit me!!! I love chains!"

The leather enthusiast pulled the back of his tight black leather vest up and bent over. As he backed up towards the leading man,

"Give it to me baby! I love chains!"

The entire squad of police jumped on the bent over leather enthusiast, possibly to his joy. He was lead away while continuing various other requests.

The English director approached the two of us, as if we stole biscuits from the cookie jar. He whispered,

"Please…remove your rehearsals from under the illumination."

We got the shot after 3am in Greenwich Village.

As the sunrise brought a halt to the festivities, we wrapped the shoot and I headed for aspirin. Before I caught a cab, I saw, on the street, a body of black leather sound asleep against the wood of a street police barricade. With his head on the wooden pillow, he finally looked at peace. I guess we all had quite an evening.

LESSON LEARNED

If you hear the reassurance of others, it is a sign that there is already a threat to your well-being. In the end, it is up to you to protect yourself.

CUT!

One crisp April late afternoon in Manhattan, I walked up the subway stairs onto Madison Avenue. I was to report to our movie location at a large office building up the street. They were engaged in shooting an exterior movie scene at the entrance to this building and I arrived, having a late call time.

Trouble often starts with "I was walking along minding my own business." A small group of excited men huddled by the edge of a building. They surrounded an upside down cardboard box. Behind the box, stood a Latino man, with a complexion like the surface of the moon. He sported a thin mustache that was maybe dunked in mascara. His eyes never remained still, always raking the half circle of cackling men, or searching the street up and down. This is not a good sign of character.

A wad of money was trapped between the fingers of his left hand. Three playing cards, curved in their middles, were in a line on top of the cardboard box, serving as a makeshift street table. I recognized this game of chance.

The game is called 3-card Monte on the street. It is a con game in which a crooked but skilled dealer assisted by one or two shills (assistants in the con) separate "the mark" from their hard earned money. One card is typically the red queen of hearts (why is it always a female with a big red heart?) and the remaining two cards are black cards like clubs or spades. These three cards are sorted and moved slowly in a deceptively clear easy manner. Everyone feels they know which face down card is the red one. One of the shills throws down a $20 bill and picks the correct card. The cards are now shifted like before and "The Mark" is fished in to win like the other guy just did. The Mark does not detect a quick skilled move this time and instead of a sure win, they lose their bet. Cheated by the con.

In business, this is called "easy money." All the recipe calls for is greed.

Should any police happen along, all that is required of this going street enterprise is to kick the cardboard box and walk away.

As I passed this scam, I witnessed a Mark losing his $20 bill. His eyes boiled like eggs and he became very still and very quiet.

At the corner of the block, a much larger crowd was gathered. The movie I "was on" was shooting a scene at the entrance of a large office building that served as our location. The shot was at one of those large areas sheltered by the building, before you enter the revolving doors to the lobby.

Our movie crew surrounded the two stars, in a scene where one character was interviewing the other, as if for the eyewitness news, plus, a local real TV news crew was present taping a segment on the movie shoot. Our fine British director was beside the big 35mm Panavision movie camera. Between our movie film camera and the two stars, was an open foreground space for the picture. Cameras were rolling and all was silent among the surrounding half circle of movie crew, TV eyewitness news crew, and onlookers watching the shoot.

All of a sudden, without warning, a man's piercing scream was heard at the edge of the side of the crowd. People were violently knocked aside by two men bursting through the crowd. The screaming man was none other than the Latin dealer of the 3-card Monte game. The man chasing him was "the mark," who was now a fireball of blind rage. Even if one does not speak Spanish, the meaning of the screaming language needed no movie subtitles.

Into the empty space between the "A-Camera" and our two leading actor stars, crashed the two struggling men. The dealer was now getting the worst of the deal, with the mark on top of him. The two stars, our English director, the movie crew, the local news team, and some assorted onlookers, stood motionless in time.

The screaming mark grabbed a healthy handful of the dealer's black hair and jerked his head up, gloriously exposing the tempting curve of the neck below.

Of all things to pull next, the Mark pulled out an old fashioned straight edged barber's razor. 20th Century Fox could not have chosen a scarier prop. He thumbed the shiny razor blade out and raised it ceremoniously in preparation to slit the dealer's throat. Imagine that for an "ow-wee." The crowd now added movie sound and screamed right on real-life cue.

For the first time, the mark fell to distraction (read your lessons on distraction in this book). He broke his focus (doing one thing at a time fully). The deadly mark looked up and saw all of the shocked witness pool. To make it more of a difficult scene for him, he saw that he was being recorded live on eyewitness news and additionally on 35mm Panavision motion picture film.

Without so much as a bow, the mark's rage seemed to have lifted. He experienced a moment of clarity. Without finishing his surgery on the crooked dealer, he ran for it. He busted through the two now non-verbal stars and tore into the revolving doors of the building. The Latin dealer seemed to disappear into the chaos of the screaming crowd.

Our movie filming had an unscheduled recess, while police searched the building for the apprentice barber. He and the card shark were never found.

This incident not only made the 6 o'clock news, but it was also written up in the N.Y. Times. Our distinguished English movie director pointed out to the media, that when the razor was lifted up, it would have been quite improper to yell—

"CUT!"

LESSON LEARNED

In the middle of a big deal, when everything suddenly blows up in your face, there is a tendency to be at a loss for words.

15 Hours from Midnight

My M.O.S. (Military Occupational Specialty) was 97Bravo40—Counter-Intelligence Agent. With this specialized M.O.S., I could only be assigned to the intelligence field. The price to pay is that I can technically be recalled to active duty for the rest of my life. Maybe the reason for this is if I spilled too many of the beans at the ripe age of one hundred years old, I could be recalled to active duty and helped into a geriatric military court martial chair.

Advanced individual training (AIT) was at the Ft. Holabird Intelligence School in Baltimore, which I believe also served secretly to guard key witnesses in very hairy federal cases. After my graduation from the Army's smallest post, I was assigned to a field office in the 115th M.I. Group.

I first had to meet and stand before the group's regional commander. This C.O. (Commanding Officer) was a Lt. Colonel and after I saluted and was given a seat, I did what I now coach others to do in meeting and interviewing.

I respectfully connected with my superior across the desk and appropriately disarmed my personality. I then broke the ice and relaxed more by relaxing him. I dropped all pretense, still maintaining the chain of command, and opened up the beginning of a genuine relationship for whatever I was to face in the conversation.

My new C.O. recognized my lack of stiffness and ease. He took interest in me. While sharing my background, my interest in acting came out. That was "the key" between us. The Lt. Colonel loved his past in acting. So much so, he wanted to go back to acting after his upcoming retirement from active duty. We were no longer strangers meeting and interviewing. We had relationship.

This successful business interview and meeting caused the regional C.O. to remember me well. So well, that he specifically chose me "the actor agent" for a special assignment in a deep undercover operation.

An M.I. counter-intelligence agent has a broad spectrum of possible duty assignments, such as background investigation for top secret security clearances, undercover security operations, surveillance, executive protection (V.I.P. bodyguard), interrogation, and there was even training in defense against methods of entry (lock picking) and sound (bugging). I was requested for a type of undercover operation conveniently called a "penetration exercise."

Once upon a time, there may have existed a small depot hiding ammunition and explosives located in the middle of nowhere in the barren desert of this continental United States (CONUS). Maybe there were other "thingamajigs" stored underground that were much more powerful than even the highest of explosives.

It would be in poor taste to store those "thingamajigs" near your neighborhood, where one boom could relocate you to another planet. So this calls for the very best security we can muster.

In the practice of physical security, the smaller the area to protect—the better. If you wish to protect valuables in your home, your entire home may have a delaying mechanism such as an alarm. But the actual hardcore protection of your valuables must be concentrated in a much smaller area for greater protection.

This little depot was so proudly protected, it had never once had its security broken. So highly thought of was this hidden cache, that three to four times a year attempts to penetration exercise a breach in their security were given their best by M.I. agents. Never once did an undercover penetration exercise succeed. The fruit of these operations was that every person working in the depot was on full time lookout for any "spooks" (intelligence slang for spies).

If that is not enough, this place was established during World War II to move inland from the Pacific coast and the hands of the Japanese. That makes Special Agent Sakamoto the frosting on the cake.

This is how agent actor was called to a field office four hours drive from the target. I was to report in uniform cover to the field office C.O., who would brief me on the super plan their covert minds had hatched.

By the way, this was the only time that I wore my uniform while on active duty after basic training and A.I.T. Now, I was supposed to act like a soldier.

I sat before the Major in charge of the field office. I wondered why I did not have more than an hour of briefing. The brass welcomed me and laid it out,

"For the first time, our plan calls for a double penetration."

I started to wince but managed to catch it fast. What?

"Yes sir." I grunted. He rolled on,

"Another team of two agents will pose as surveyors outside the perimeter of the depot." He awaited my response,

"They won't live long and prosper, sir."

"Of course not. Once a set of real drug enforcement credentials was dropped out of a helicopter onto the high security area. If that didn't work, this certainly won't. It's not supposed to work. Do you see where this is going agent?"

"Yes sir. Those two agent surveyors get busted right away. Happy ending."

The Major smiled with pride and continued,

"You are to report in the night before at midnight, as a Vietnam returning Specialist 4 clerk typist. You just finished your tour at Da Nang base camp."

My eye twitched "ouch." I respectfully brought up,

"Sir. I've never been to Da Nang."

"Well, I have. What do you want to know?"

"How much time do we have Sir?"

"I will be leaving in 30 minutes."

Terrific. Given all the time in the world to go over my cover, I had to improvise,

"Sir. What is the oddest thing about Da Nang Base?"

At first he studied my seriousness, then a memory cooperated,

"The Chinese restaurant on base. It is the safest structure to run to when mortar fire is incoming."

"Thank you Sir. That is exactly the type of info I need."

"You have from midnight to the following afternoon. You will terminate this exercise at 1500 hours (300pm)."

"So I have 15 hours from midnight. To make a breach in their security for the first time in history."

"Affirmative."

I could see that was all the slack I would get. I tried to wiggle my ears.

"Sir. Anything else to keep in mind?"

"Negative. Do the best you can. The colonel told me you are—the—man. An actor."

I collected my false orders and papers. It was late in the afternoon when the closing field office kicked me out.

It was a couple of hours later when I reached a casino half way to my target. I should not have stopped. But I justified a much deserved break to eat a little sandwich. There would be no chow to eat at midnight. Also, it was too early to arrive at the target. So I decided to rest for a while at the roulette table. That was permissible since I never win. (Denial = rationalizing, justifying, excusing)

When I was a kid, all I wanted was to take a drink legally and be able to walk into a casino. Today, I have not had a drink in over 28 years and I have come to despise gambling.

But…at that time, I pulled up a stool to the wheel of fortune. I started to play six numbers at a time. Unfortunately, I got lucky.

As I started to win, a kind pretty lady brought me a slug of scotch, on the house. The more chips I won, the more I ran into this kind pretty lady posing as a free scotch dispenser. A jovial crowd of merrymakers began to gather around my roulette table. I looked down at my big stack of colorful chips. I then experienced a moment of clarity. I was getting drunk. And I seemed to remember that I had someplace important to be at midnight.

I somehow managed to escape the pit boss, the kind lady, and the arms of my newfound merrymaking friends. I busted out of that casino in a somewhat sideways manner. I was too tipsy to drive and too dull to penetrate the exercise.

I was getting my bearings, when I spotted the bright lights of a movie theater across the street. Its movie marquee was an epiphany—PAINT YOUR WAGON. I now knew how to recover. I spent the next hours with Clint Eastwood and Lee Marvin singing me into sobriety.

Nothing is as dark as the dark desert. I reached the perimeter wired fence of the target area at 12 midnight. I had a headache and a fine case of cotton mouth.

I could just find the main gate and report in like a civilized person. But no. I only had 15 hours more, so let's open up for business.

I looked for a place to maybe drive through the fence. Not like gangbusters, but maybe there was an opening I could find. My car headlights were a tiny pool in the darkness of the black air. The bitterness of sagebrush tickled my nostrils. Let the adventure begin.

I didn't get far. There is something unmistakable about flashing red and blue lights, especially when speeding right at you. I was treated to a blinding spotlight frying my eyeballs. I stopped the car and got out with my empty hands in plain sight.

The security truck screeched to a halt. I waved a merry "hello" into the blindness of the spotlight beam. As I waved and smiled, I yelled,

"Am I glad to see you!"

In business, when you get caught red handed, it is best to act a bit stupid. The one who caught you will feel more at ease in the discussion soon to follow. I continued to "whistle in the dark,"

"I need your help."

Keep the other person on top of you.

"I got lost. Hello?"

I heard the truck doors opening. Two armed helmeted uniforms carefully approached me. One was on each edge of the spotlight beam. One shadow spoke,

"What are you doing out here?"

Very friendly and even stupider.

"I'm reporting as ordered. Here are my orders."

I very slowly lifted the phony papers. Helmet #1 took them from me. As he read, I blabbed on,

"I just got back. I got lost. It's dark out here. I sure am glad to see you guys."

Helmet #2 moved near my side. I made sure he got a good whiff of my breath with a "Phhhhhh". He popped,

"You been drinkin'?"

I countered right away,

"Yes and no."

"What you mean yes and no?"

That was my cue,

"Yes I had a drink. No I haven't been drinking."

That broke the ice. They chuckled and I built on it,

"I stopped at that big Casino on the way here. A lady with a drink tray took all my coin."

The ice melted more moving from a glacier to an ice cube. The two helmets nodded with laughter.

"Yup. They got my pay too."

Helmet #1 handed me back my fake orders that looked real.

"Follow us into the Main Gate. We'll show you where to report to."

I was escorted to the C.Q. (Charge of Quarter), who wiped the sleep crust out of his eye. With tired routine, he assigned me to a temporary bed. I also was issued a temporary place to eat and a time to report to the admin building in the morning. I wanted an early start, as the clock was ticking away fast.

At sunup, I innocently drove around the depot unrestricted areas. I had a lot of scouting to do before I had to report in to admin. The set up was simple, like all good things that actually work. I was in the low level security areas around the perimeter of the base. Within this circle was a smaller area surrounded by a lot of physical security fences and armed guards. Within that inner high security circle would be another much smaller area of the highest restricted circle. The grand prize. Getting past the next level of armed guards, alarm towers, and voltage fences would be an interesting challenge for any secret agent. I had 15 hours from midnight and half of the time was now gone.

I straggled into the admin building late and it was now time for the acting curtain to rise. My emotional choice was I felt sad and regretful for reporting late. If I needed to, I would throw in a little more dumb and nervous. If someone asks you for your papers, they will read it to justify their command.

If you shove your papers at them, they will not like your intrusion and maybe only glance at them. Everyone bought my bogus orders and papers. Of course, they were well forged.

There was amused gossip going around about how "two of those spooky spies" got caught this morning trying to pose as surveyors. It would be nice if this turned into arrogance. I was ordered to report to Chief Warrant officer Washington, down the hall.

Warrant officer is a great rank in the army. It is a respected grade somewhere between master sergeant and officer. Warrant officers have all the privileges of an officer and not the overall responsibility. They are all career "lifers." They are addressed properly as "Mister." Chief warrant officers and senior sergeants run the machinery of the army.

The old wooden room was small and tidy. I studied it quickly. It was used to a lot of work and traffic. A huge heavy metal government desk split the small room; framed proud pictures of grandchildren sat on display.

Chief warrant officer Washington was at home behind the gunmetal desk. He was a latter middle-aged African-American with a neat pencil mustache trimmed to perfection. His uniform was career starched and fit well over his small frame. It only took this long to determine who ran the procedures of this base.

The Chief welcomed me with a soft but firm voice. There was a slight trace of accent and there was a slight glottal stop when speaking, which I made a mental note of. He smiled with the warmth of an old friend.

"Specialist 4 Sakamoto." In warm greeting, "Please have a seat."

There was no doubt in my mind, he was a sly fox, maybe Texas originally. I settled in the government chair, sitting at attention. He looked into my soul (great connection and relationship established immediately) Now comes the time to speak under pressure.

"Welcome."

"Thank you sir." I tagged along.

"Everyone calls me Mistah."

"Yes sir. Mister Washington." Slip a little and then place him up above.

The melting of the first layer of ice drew a warm grin. He is looking into me for pretense or how I defend myself. Just disarm and let him be in charge. He studied my orders carefully, as if he was ordering dinner at an overpriced restaurant. He groaned in almost a rhythm –

"Umm humm."

More cautious study,

"Umm humm."

Without looking up at me, from out of nowhere,

"How many words a minute can you type?"

Great sly trap. Without hesitation and with a smile,

"I guess I'm about average, Mister Washington."

The Chief slowly rolled a paper into his typewriter. I was studying his profile, as he banged away on the keys with two fingers. This is now an interrogation,

"This fast?"

I shook my head, "Maybe on a good day."

He slowed to a hunt and peck. His voice rose,

"This fast?"

"Maybe on a real bad day…Mister Washington."

The Chief stopped typing and then stared at the paper. Silence. I waited for the shot. He aimed his head at me and looked at the back of my eyeballs. He then pulled the trigger on me,

"When was the last mortar attack on Da Nang? He stared at me. Hesitation would be fatal. I leaned my eyes into him and naively blurted,

"I don't remember. But they didn't get the Chinese restaurant."

We both maintained eye contact follow through and he broke first. The glacier of ice melted to a cube and a deep glottal laugh choked the Chief,

"Yah—Ah hear ya." He shook his head staring at me, "Chahneez rest'rant hah!" The phone rang with a bang.

The Chief placed the phone receiver on his left shoulder and half held it in place with his chin. I could tell this was habit. Look for habits. He answered,

"Mistah Washington here." He mumbled into the phone, "Yah. Umm Humm. Thanks."

The Chief hung up the phone and was ready to tell me something. It rang again. He picked up the receiver and placed it on his left shoulder exactly as before, with his mouth against the speaker piece. Habit confirmed.

"Mistah Washington here…Yah…Umm Humm…Thanks."

He again hung up his busy phone. The Chief held up a finger to indicate a pause. He lifted the phone receiver and dialed quickly. The receiver was held the exact same way as he mumbled,

"Mistah Washington here. Ah'm sendin'" Spec 4 Sakamoto to you. Give 'im temp quarters an' show 'im to the mess hall.

The Chief finished with assurance and in the same exact tone,

"Thanks." Everyone followed his orders. Remember that.

He hung up the phone and released me to go set up with my quarters. I was to report back that afternoon, after I got settled. I memorized the Chief's habits when he was on the phone.

I made sure that I forgot where I was supposed to go and made a beeline for the building housing the Explosive Ordinance Disposal Unit (EOD). I now had a solid plan improvised, after my meeting with the Chief.

Since EOD would have total and quick access to any restricted area, I would impersonate Chief Washington's distinctive speaking over the phone and order EOD to show me around as a new addition to their Unit.

Earlier that morning, I spied out the EOD emergency building. Buck Sergeant Dewey was the only one stuck there at top of the morning. He happily gave the directions I did not need to find the admin building. The only vehicle parked outside this small building was the emergency truck, nicely adorned with a bank of flashing lights and siren on it's cab. No armed guard would miss recognizing this big emergency vehicle.

From a phone booth near the EOD emergency building, I managed to get the exchange to connect me with this unit. I then placed the phone receiver on my shoulder and smushed the speaker onto my mouth (a la Chief Washington). I conjured up my best mellow African-American voice, including glottal stops. A snappy answer from the phone,

"EOD! Sergeant Dewey speaking, sir."

Here we go, "Mistah Washington here."

"Yes Chief!"

So far so good. Now let's run with it. I mumbled a bit, "Got a new man 'ere. Spec 4 Sakamoto."

Sergeant Dewey interrupted, "Yes sir. I helped him find you this morning."

I grunted, "Umm Humm. You need a clerk typist ta'ssist you?"

The Sergeant jumped on it, "Sure do Chief!"

Now let's close the loop, "Umm Humm. Figured. Ah' jus' sent him to you. Show him around. What you all do an' such."

The Buck Sergeant promised, "I'll give him the grand tour."

Now to polish him off, "Umm Humm—thanks."

Any sergeant would covet someone to type for them.

As I peeked into the EOD door, with just the right amount of humility, Sergeant Dewey greeted me like a brother.

"Come in, come in."

He stood posing behind his government metal desk, with a gentle authority. That is when you know a sergeant has already got you. I did not hear anyone else in the small building. I stood at attention before him,

"Specialist 4 Sakamoto reporting as ordered, sergeant."

"Fine, fine. At ease. Look Sakamoto, this unit is more relaxed. 'specially with all of the exciting work we do."

I did an imitation of a Japanese hayseed. "What work is that, sergeant?"

He glowed and leaned toward me, as if letting me know the winner of the next horse race.

"Explosive Ordinance Disposal."

I gulped, "I don't like getting blown up. I guess I'm not as brave as you guys."

"No, no! It's all cool. I'll show you. Let's go on the grand tour."

"Can we go in that cool truck of yours?"

The sergeant gave me a thumbs up. "Maybe we'll light it up and hit the siren."

"When? Now?"

"Let me fetch the keys."

Once I got him alone in the truck, I could come up with some way to get into the innermost highest restricted area. I only needed to get near there for a moment and the security would be considered breached.

As we were merrily heading out the door, the phone gave a fatal ring. Fatal phone calls have a particular ring. Sergeant Dewey answered the call,

"EOD! Sergeant Dewey speaking, sir."

I didn't like the silence. The sergeant listened carefully with the intensity of life or death directions. He then snapped,

"Yes sir! I'll get the team over immediately."

He slammed the phone receiver down and spoke without looking at me.

"We got an emergency condition. See you later on."

He stormed out the door. I was left holding my cute plan in my empty hands. The scream of the siren pulling away woke me up to how we always work with time, but a single moment can make it decisive.

I had no time for "if only" pondering and less time for lunch. I had to improvise another plan of action. How am I going to deal with this now?

I settled on the main gate to the next level high security area. The sentry box at the gate was manned by only one armed security guard, waving both entrance and exit lanes to move through the blockade gate. I did not like going against an armed middle-aged private security guard. Anything could happen under panic. I would have much preferred a highly trained Marine. But acceptance is easy when you have no choice.

It was just before 12 noon and the blockade gates were lifted up for the lunch rush of traffic. That gate would have created a huge traffic jam at that hour, if it had to go up and down for each vehicle. So my plan was to run the gate with the returning lunch traffic heading back into the restricted area. I studied the gates in hidden surveillance and noticed that when one car was going out and one car was coming back, the guard had no time to really check the driver's flashing ID. I would exploit that opportunity.

Just before lunch hour ended, my car joined the fleet returning back from lunch. I had my Military Intelligence (MI) badge and credentials in my top left shirt pocket. As I approached the gate, I removed my credentials and placed my left thumb over the top. I played my brakes to time going through the gate just as a car going out would be on the other side of the solo guard. This exiting car was waved on and the armed guard turned quickly towards my car. I made sure I looked him in the eyes (connection), smiled big (relationship) and held up my MI credentials. Steadily and slowly, I rolled through the entrance towards the restricted area. The guard's hand moved on it's own (habit) and waved me into the area. I was in.

I checked the rear view mirror for a gun barrel and incoming fire. No such thing, just an overworked armed guard waving at cars right and left. Now where?

Since I was now in the restricted security area of the base, I may as well go for finding the highest restricted area. All I had to do was follow the high voltage fence. There had to be an entrance somewhere.

I am not Olympic at pole-vaulting high voltage fences, so I parked near a guardhouse to an inner area. I saw people walking into this area displaying their IDs.

I joined the parade and walked with the people whose tummies were full of lunch. I held up my MI badge and credential as I passed another middle-aged armed guard. He motioned us in. I did not look back. I could hear the dirt under my shoes.

I must have lasted about ten yards and then heard an unmistakable sharp,

"Halt!"

Everyone stopped in their tracks. I turned with great curiosity. The guard with the gun wanted to chat with me. One hand pointed to me and the other hand rested on his holstered Smith and Wesson Model 10 38 special revolver. I chose not to look stupid. I chose to look like an "officer and a gentleman." Which for me, was quite a stretch. I marched up to the not so relaxed armed guard, not displaying my credentials. I could read some fear and confusion in his eyes. He was firm,

"Wait here sir."

The guard returned to the guardhouse and jerked up the phone receiver.

He turned his back. It was time for me to dash.

By the time I started up my car, the wail of sirens screamed into the air. I casually drove back towards the main gate, as I noticed more and more flashing lights. The only thing missing was diving aircraft.

There was confusion at the main gate I previously ran. I followed an exiting car. It must have been my waving hand that inspired our reunion. The gate was down and not moving for me. The armed guard held one hand up in "Halt" and the other hand joined Smith and Wesson. His eyes betrayed a somewhat different relationship, like when a woman says "We need to talk." I heard a well projected male voice,

"Stop the car!"

I did so. Not exactly out of willingness. The guard carried on,

"Now get out of the car. Keep your hands where I can see them!"

I did so without adding any social comment on his abruptness. He carried on,

"Turn around and face the car. Put your hands on the car. Now spread your feet."

As I complied, I remember seeing the clear blue desert sky. All I could think about was how I did my duty and was about to get shot by my own side.

As I assumed "the position," the guard's fingers frisked me for weapons. Somehow he missed my badge and credentials in my upper left shirt pocket. I was running out of time in more ways than one. I was hooked up (handcuffed) and hauled off with escort. Plus, I had completely missed lunch.

There are times in business when an interview slips into an interrogation. And there are times when an interrogation slips into being surrounded by seven scary security chiefs. The leader of which had one eye. Every time he stared at me I felt like he was taking aim.

The seven deadly sins drilled into me with their eyes. The silence reminded me of when my elementary school principal captured me in her office. Silence. These men were becoming dangerous. I began to regret all of the soon to be wasted money my parents had spent on braces straightening out my teeth, which in a moment would be smiling from the floor.

They grilled me in the third degree. I stuck with my innocent naïve "my dog ate my homework." After the fourth and fifth degree and my unwavering simple story of getting lost and stuck in the flow of lunch traffic—somehow, someway—I talked my way out of it and raised a shadow of a doubt. My father said I'd make a good mouthpiece of a lawyer. The seven security chiefs did not lock me up or rearrange my face. They gave me a reprieve to return to my barracks for now.

The seven stood up en masse and turned to leave. I glanced at the government clock on the wall. It read 1445 hours, only 15 more minutes left until termination of this penetration exercise.

I thought of making a final run for it, but that might end up terminating me. Always ask yourself—do I really need to bleed? Especially when it is drawn from my own side. What is about to happen will be dangerous enough.

As the seven interrogators headed toward the door, I moved behind a convenient steel government desk for protection. I removed my MI badge and credentials from my upper left shirt pocket. There is an earth shaking sound when a badge lands on a metal desk. That piercing "clink" stopped the seven security chiefs in their tracks. Slowly they turned to the unexpected sound. To ward off the upcoming violence, in very rapid fire, I raised my arms in praise,

"You are good! You...gentlemen!...are so good! Really-really good!"

The leader with the one eye coughed at me,

"So are you."

Thus terminated 15 hours from midnight. For the first time in their history, the security of this base had been breached. I later found out that my brief visit and fanciful story-telling caused chaos exploding in Washington D.C., Saigon, and Department of the Army. Everybody was trying to hunt me down.

As for me, I deserved a reward. Don't you agree? So I gave myself orders to go AWOL (Absent Without Leave) for a day and get lost in the shuffle. The shuffle back at the big casino. Maybe that nice lady with the tray would still be there.

Let the chips fall where they may.

LESSON LEARNED

Just like a battle, your real-life situation is constantly fluid and changes moment to moment. Your survival and success depends on how you receive what is in front of you and adapt without hesitation, never losing the importance of your goal. Never expect anything—never anticipate anything— never know what is going to happen and you will not be thrown off. Look for an opening to disrupt the other person with surprise. My understanding of the wisdom of the great boxer Mike Tyson : "No plan survives a punch in the mouth." Deal with whatever is in front of you wholeheartedly. Let others worry and hold back.

I'll Have Trouble on the Rocks... With a Twist

Bartender. Now there is another fantasy profession. A bedrock for social chat. I would need "a trade" to pay the rent when I journeyed to NYC to become an actor. Like many brainstorms while bar drinking, this seemed to be a good idea at the time.

I searched for lessons from my favorite bartenders. Here is a summary of customer service and speaking under social pressure,

"Don't pay any attention to what they say. When they look sad and shake their head—you look sad and shake your head. When they look happy and nod their head—you look happy and nod your head. When you want to get away from them, just start laughing as if they said something clever and wise and then walk away."

So I thought I should attend a small bartender's school. We practiced making drinks that you would only get an order for once in a blue moon at the swankiest of dinner houses. How about a drink called "Between the Sheets?"

I got my first bartending job in a neighborhood joint serving drinks for an adjacent pancake house. I realized later that I was hired specifically for being a dummy. As a first time green bartender, the overworked pancake manager could use me to take a Sunday night off with his family and not worry about being stolen blind. All he needed was someone with no experience stealing, who could pour a shot, and count to 20. A far cry from mixing a "Golden Fizz."

I showed up to my first job "behind the stick" in a clean white dress shirt and black vest. The pancake manager helped me up onto the duckboards behind the bar and bid me "good luck." My only directions were:

"Just leave all the money in the register. I'll count out tomorrow morning."

He then rushed out before I could run away.

The bar was a horseshoe shaped bar. The only worse bar to work is a full circle bar, without any direction to safely point your back. There were a lot of stools and everyone was practicing how to get drunk. I must have arrived late at the party. The bar manager was there. He was practicing breathing down brandy and soda (not taught in bartender school). The only thing he was managing was the giggling woman hanging on to him. You know it is bad when you slur your giggles.

There was a pool table in a side alcove to my left. I never drank in bars with pool tables, as they attract a different class of patrons.

Then came the gambling initiation. Before I could pour my first drink, I was challenged by house rules to toss dice against the bar manager himself. The dice game is called "boss dice" and it requires two dice cups, each holding six dice.

You slam the cups onto the bar three different times and the best hand wins. The bet in the bar was double or nothing. If the customer wins, the drinks are free. If the bartender wins, the customer pays double. My first challenge was drinks for the entire bar, who did their best screaming and cheerleading.

At this point, we should probably examine the concept of gambling. Business and life are full of taking risks if you do it right. Gambling, especially if it is compulsive, I have come to despise. I have seen it get violent and ugly from dives to exclusive clubs. It can become a dark spell cast over anyone who falls under it.

I have been friendly with a couple of folks who owned old-fashioned legal card rooms. They survived by knowing the odds and more so by knowing people and what they do under pressure.

One card room owner, for kicks, took vacations helping the Drug Enforcement Administration (DEA). In their old family run card room, he and his brother took on all comers. At his card table, he considered himself to be a reincarnation of Doc Holliday (marshal Wyatt Earp's killer friend from the gunfight at the OK Corral on 26 October 1881). He kept a 22 magnum cowboy style revolver with him when he dealt cards. He sat on it. Some like to keep their gun near their jewels.

I asked this salty pro gambler, how he could survive playing cards so much and not average out losing. His business advice was steady,

"Three things to remember –

One poker is a game of ego.

Two you must never let money be the most important thing to you.

Three when the big bet comes—look into the other person. Most people will give themselves away."

Just to make things crystal clear, if you are a person who likes to gamble, that is none of my business.

Meanwhile back to the pancake saloon. Everyone in the bar now had a backup drink. Just what they needed. I tossed against the bar manager.

I still remember what was going on through me because I usually did not toss dice. Most of the time, I lost at gambling. But that perspective of hesitation, worry, doubt—did not enter my head. Without distraction of money, I just picked up the dice cup and began to do it, without thought.

I wiped out the bar manager with an incredible hand of dice. He paid double with surprise and amusement. I did not win with skill, just action without doubt.

With a roar, the entire bar challenged me to a dice duel. Drinks for the entire house at double or nothing became "what's next."

I beat everyone, one at time, in short order. Not from expertise, but rather from empty headed boldness not caring at all about winning. Drinks lined up the bar until I ran out of glasses. It is just as well. The motley collection drank itself to tire, as the stools became hazardous and the conversations lost their brilliance. So faded the sad torch songs from the jukebox.

After I moved to NYC, I jumped from pancakes to the pie in the sky, Radio City Music Hall. The one and only.

Radio City, show place of our nation and home of the dancing Rockettes, was once the top tourist attraction in the Big Apple. Sometime around 1974, it hit the hardest of times. Financially it was busted and there was even talk of the famous French oceanographer turning it into some kind of aquarium. Efforts to preserve the grand old venue became desperate.

Someone got the bright idea to rent to promoters of live music tours. That is how Rhythm & Blues (R&B) first came to Radio City Music Hall.

About a dozen bartenders were hired to serve three mezzanines with men's room on one side and women's room on the other. Three bartenders would work the main bar in the lobby and three handled the lower floor where the main floor restrooms were located.

We were hired for this gig by a partnership of two streetwise NYC bar and restaurant owners. One was a tall lanky Irish former golden gloves boxer, from the Bronx. And the other was a short fiery Jewish hip dresser from the corner. They were city tough but good guys in my book. They knew how to stay calm under fire.

We all had one meeting before the first sold out show. Again, these were not Rockette performances. They booked the top R&B stars and sold out every plush seat in Radio City. We were to sell drinks before the show and during a twenty minute or so intermission. To expedite each bar station, all drinks were mixed from "the well" priced at $1.75 each and $1 for a soda. Each bartender would ring up the money in a small cash register behind the temporary small bar stand.

No one had a clue of what to expect. We were told the capacity was around 5,000 seats. I don't know. Someone would be making a lot of cash. We were paid a shift wage in cash and no one expected tips.

After our orientation meeting, a tall hip young bartender approached me,

"Goin' ta' da' train?"

That is a New York question. You leave out the subject and make it a question by raising your voice inflection higher as you speak. If it was more important or urgent you would say,

"Goin' ta' da' train aw wut?"

He was not curious. He was smart. In NYC odds, two going to the subway at night are better than one. Smart ones are careful and have a longer life span.

Because of my experience, I was given the opening night anticipated hot spot for traffic, which was by the first mezzanine lady's room.

The ball opened as the grand doors of main floor swung open for a new wave of concert patrons. A mob stormed in and rushed to secure their seating, as if they could not trust the tickets.

There was not much interest in purchasing beverages prior to the show. There were a lot of bulges in clothing. Someone was in such a rush, they dropped a 38 caliber cartridge on the plush carpet next to my station. Perhaps there was a lot of unwinding from the subway commute, as there seemed to be a lot of "lighting up" funny shaped cigarettes. The loud crowd rocked with the music and all was calm at our bar station until the fateful intermission.

When the mezzanine doors swung open for the intermission, a cloud of marijuana smoke billowed out so thick you could cut it up and bag it. Hundreds of stoned music lovers rushed out of the gas chamber and headed right at me and the rest-rooms. For the next twenty minutes, I did what is known in the bar business as "buried my head in the ice." Not only did I get slammed making drinks, but I also had to make change for every drink sold. That makes it ripe for con artist thieves.

Here is how you make change facing the crooked. It is so easy for a con to claim they gave you a $20 bill instead of a $5 bill. They just choose a time when you are so busy, it is possible to make an error in change. So I stop this by "facing the money." After I receive the payment, I turn all bills up with the dead President's face in the same direction. Then when I put the bill facing the same way into the drawer, I leave the drawer clip in the up position, while I hand back the change. This means that I have examined the bill three times and have the backup of the bill in the drawer designated with the drawer clip. No crook will miss this. I have never been challenged on giving the wrong change. If you take care of your business and they see you are that cautious with the money, the crooks will move on to fleece another sheep.

After the bar owners told the other NYC bartenders about my handling of the money, I heard one of them crack in typical New York manner,

"Ya hiyah' bout da' guy. All 'iz money faces north."

Further notoriety came later when during one show, I was decorated by the bar owners as the fastest bartender in the city. At $1.75 a drink, I took in a total of $1,100. This legend would later get me a job at an "Upper East Side Disco."

The bartender on the other side of the first mezzanine did not fare so well. His station came under attack by the goblins. It seems that in the height of the rush, a squad of gang teens worked him. While the bartender was pulled away with a distraction, other goblins grabbed his cash register and ran away with it. He yelled for help but the money was long gone, leaving his empty cash register near the stylish Radio City door exit. Welcome to downtown.

Not being the only goblin attack, the furious bar owners vowed to get security for us.

So the next evening, I looked down from the first mezzanine and saw in the lobby a platoon of uniformed security guards. That is to say a platoon of geriatric uniformed security guards. They were unarmed and had a small police baton hanging from their belts (the kind the keystone cops used in the silent movies). The Irish boxer bar owner came to me and loudly complained,

"Look at that security! My old lady could security more than that."

The other careful subway bartender whispered to me,

"Dose geezers got bats – kiddin' me aw wut!"

I received added help from a bar boy, who was recruited from a tough Irish neighborhood. He was about 15 years old and sported clothes he had long ago outgrown. To compensate, he was a very big tough kid who did not mind "throwing blows" with anybody. I confided to the big lumbering teen, "Keep the cups iced. And watch out for me when I go down for the ice."

He comforted me without an abundance of feelings, "Yeah."

Though the evening went without further incident, the security guards earned a well-deserved trip back into retirement.

What security came next seemed more out of a desire for revenge. New York has a way of dubbing individuals with a new but concise name. The next security for protecting us and the grand old Radio City was crowned,

"The Karate Guys."

No badges. Just chops and kicks. They were a platoon of young men who liked to fight. Period. End of qualifications. As they say in NYC, "end a' staw-ree."

The leader of "The Karate Guys" was a Chinese man, who looked like a descendant of the god of good luck you see in Chinatown souvenir stores. One time he pulled out a Colt Cobra 38 snub nosed revolver from his ankle holster. Unprofessionally, he let the gun muzzle point at me. I sharply pointed out,

"Watch out where you point that."

He smirked,

"No pwoblem. Loaded wi' shot."

That means the god of good luck had 38 special cartridges loaded with tiny birdshot instead of bullets. This type of cartridge is meant for crawling snakes and I don't mean the two-legged variety. Great. The party was on.

Soon afterwards, Radio City had the privilege of a concert from "The Queen." I had the further privilege of meeting and working with her head bodyguard. As he could do nothing when she was onstage, he and his assistant made a few extra bucks guarding our stations on the first mezzanine during the intermission onslaught.

I got to know this bodyguard. There is no one so calm as a big strong African-American with Black Belts in Judo and the Tomiki style of Aikido. He learned these martial arts while serving in Japan and taught kids living "in the ghetto," as it was called then. Under his left arm hung a large frame Smith & Wesson Model 27 357 magnum loaded with 125 grain hollow point bullets. His chest was so big, he could conceal this huge revolver. I later found out from his assistant that he had used the gun twice before on the street, finalizing social encounters.

Prior to becoming bodyguards, these two men had an armored car business through the Bedford-Stuyvesant area of 1960's Brooklyn. Their armored bank car got into more than one running gun battle on those mean streets.

I asked him of his opinion of the karate guys. He was polite and soft spoken in his martial arts and business advice,

"Karate is okay. But you need to keep your balance. In a real fight, the one who ends up on the ground first will likely be the one to lose."

It did not take long before a brawl broke loose on the elegant thick plush carpet of the Radio City Music Hall lobby. I looked down from the mezzanine and saw a bunch of the karate guys exchanging punches and kicks with a gang of teen hoodlums. Radio City had turned into the Roman Colosseum, with gladiators.

I called the uninterested bodyguard over, proclaiming in honor of Caesar,

"There's a fight down there."

The big man strolled over with calmness and then took a peek down.

He appeared as if some dog had pooped on the carpet below. Turning away unimpressed, he corrected me,

"That's not a fight."

I rechecked the two idiot gangs beating on each other and then had to ask,

"That's not a fight?"

He taught me like an algebra teacher,

"That's an argument. A fight is where one person doesn't get up again."

And that is how R&B came to Radio City Music Hall.

LESSON LEARNED

When under the influence of a substance, eventually the worst will come out in people. This is especially true when in a group, which is a civilized way of saying "a pack." When the fear is lit, it will be like pouring gasoline on a fire. Pay no attention to bragging or male bravado. Those determined individuals, who keep their head when under fire, will likely walk away from the fight.

And a Slice of the Big Apple

As I said before, my speaking coaching is the culmination of my experiences.

There was another type of New York City business entrepreneur who frequented the disco clubs. This group of businessmen had been recently featured in a movie about a Godfather. Except these men were no movie. Between the hours of about 1am to 3am, there were usually two types of these entrepreneurs.

One type was a quiet reserved careful man in a very expensive jacket with no tie (kind of like Silicon Valley attire). He was always accompanied by a many times larger man who was quite non-verbal. He did look around a lot. The well-dressed man paid from a plain fat envelope removed from his inside jacket pocket. Or, he paid from a huge wad of money wrapped with a large rubber band. You can always tell when a man really has real money. He keeps the smaller bills on the outside of the wad of cash. Those who keep big bills on the outside may wish to impress.

These two men routinely had only one drink during their brief visit. Never drunk, they always seemed interested in counting heads in the room. Maybe they were assisting the census.

There was always an impressive tip left quietly for the bartender, left without fanfare, as if they had forgotten the money.

This seemingly nice arrangement can easily eventually head into a speaking under pressure very sticky predicament.

Once, a man with a nickname (they prefer nicknames) and I were on friendly terms at the bar. One friendly evening, he inquired almost indirectly, "You wanna' make some extra money?"

I had dreaded the coming of this moment of casual friendship. I coughed out,

"How is that?"

He looked away from me, "Driving a truck. One time."

As he studied me, I wiggled,

"Can I get back to you?"

I asked some advice of a few knowledgeable souls and they were firm,

"Be careful. It's all up to you. Good luck."

As they say in the Big Apple, "End a' staw-ree."

The time came for my business offer answer. I looked him in the eyes (connect) and said sincerely (relationship),

"I respect and appreciate your offer. But I'm no good with a truck."

He looked into me without expression then grinned and quipped,

"Fuh – gedda – boud – it."

Some business needs to end with a free drink and a large tip.

I transferred downstairs to the disco service bar, dealing with only the cocktail waitresses. The early 70's were the height of the disco era. If you wish to get in the mood while reading this, go to your music app and play a little of "I'll Be Around" by The Spinners, or something like that.

In the disco, you will meet the second type of heavy-duty entrepreneur at the bar. They usually do not come in pairs—they come in crews. The leaders are, shall we say, like lower management. They will bring with them the team. Usually the uniform for the day is dark expensive leather jackets. On certain occasions, management might wear sharp jackets with open shirts and a pinky ring.

An exciting moment in customer service was brought on when; a crew bellied up to the bar. Swift service was demanded. Everyone carelessly tossed out a $100 bill (known in NYC as "a yard") on the bar, demanding that I take the money they threw out to pay for all of the drinks. Here is a moment in customer service not covered in training. It was neither subtle nor quiet. It was laced with threats.

So whose money would you take? You better not look in the least bit scared. That is what they will spot immediately and you will not get paid. This is no time for hesitation, worry, or doubt. These are men of action. So here is what you do. You connect with your entire audience. You have a welcoming relationship. Do not take the money of the one yelling the loudest and threatening, which will lead to a very unpleasant consequence. These employees are known as the "hitters." How is that for a job description? You better accept and most importantly acknowledge their offer but do not take their hard earned dollars. You will spot the leader. He will not be yelling. He may even be quiet but always confident. Connect with his eyes and they will glance down at the money he tossed down. He is leading you to do it. You take his money and nod in gratitude for all to see. Do not go near the remaining money on the bar. No one else will bother it either. Money becomes so important to some people, that it loses all value. The louder ones who did not really want you to take their money will grow louder in threat about, "next time you better take mine."

As disco grew in the Big Apple, I changed jobs to a club on the upper-east side. Once again, the dance floor was packed. This club had many BBQs (Brooklyn, Bronx, Queens). There were even "immigrants" from Jersey and Connecticut. By 10pm, the line formed from the door going around the block.

Speaking of "door". This club had the best doorman/bouncer in the entire apple. He was a true pro, so much so, that he was considering the possibilities of opening up a school for bouncers called "door school." He was a huge strong Italian family man. He never looked for or wanted trouble, though he did carry a "sap" (flat blackjack) in his right sock. I only recall once when this instrument of negotiation was brought into play. Big guys usually don't look for trouble—watch out for the mean little guys. He chose to negotiate with dignity. He reasoned with drunks, troublemakers, and self-made big shots; on the wisdom of leaving. It is better business practice to stop problems before they enter your door. He was a master at receiving a tip for allowing entrance by making someone feel important. That is how guys doing door make most of the money. When he talked with you, he would be standing just a bit to your side, making it very awkward to take a swing at him.

But the key to his door actions was in firm and gentle reasoning when speaking under pressure. You get the other person to think they are joining forces with you to do what is best for all. Keep the other person from becoming an opponent (perspective and relationship) and let them form a partnership for peace and mutual benefit, as if it was their idea. He would always reason gentle and firm when speaking and then let you come to your own decision of comply and kiss the girls or kiss the sidewalk. You always felt your decision was doing everyone a favor.

I wish he had opened up "door school." He would be one of the few people I would refer you to for coaching in business tact.

Just another crunchy bite of experience from a slice of the Big Apple.

LESSON LEARNED

Violence is a part of human nature. If you think that it is only for gangs, you may mistake the danger standing right in front of you, as "He seemed like such a nice guy."

Here's How it's Really Done

Speaking Under Pressure

*Ephesians 4:29 "Do not let any unwholesome talk come
out of your mouths, but only what is helpful
for building others up according to their needs,
that it may benefit those who listen." (NIV)*

CHANGING YOUR INSIDE

Seeing Spots Before Your Very Eyes

In "Show Biz," TV commercials are called "spots," as in a "30 second spot." There is no other field of acting more relevant to business speaking, meetings, interviews, selling to strangers, or pitching, than TV commercials. That is because of their simple purposes of getting audience attention—sell the product or service—leave them wanting more.

The reason for any television dramatic, comedic, or news shows, are to hold you until the next spot.

TV commercials all try to be different, but they all use connection, relationship with the audience, and repetition (3 times is common). They are geared for the mass of people who can be influenced and there are a lot of them. Because of the limited time factor, they are a proof of the power of simplicity.

Many moons ago, TV's used to have dials to change the channels. Someone would have to get up and walk to the TV set. If they were polite or considerate, they would check with their family,

"Who wants to watch this?"

After another turn of the TV set dial, "How about this show?"

When I was a kid, our TV dial came off and I used to hide the dial when there was a show I wanted to watch.

During this long ago "golden age of television," programs used to actually have a beginning to the story. Viewers could absorb a good story with patience.

Then came the game changer. The remote control. Now control was empowered by a flick of the finger. You can now rot in your chair and go down armed with a remote in each hand. How much effect does a computer and a mouse have on the patience of people and a flick of the finger.

So what am I getting at now? Everything.

To understand today's audience—You must understand that one finger on the control or that one finger on the mouse. It has changed the whole game for everything. It has certainly done wonders concerning patience, whether viewing others on-screen or live.

Will this influence appear and disappear at times? This sense of viewing is ingrained habitually and written in concrete. Wherever you go, whatever you do, all others, can in their sub-conscious, drop their finger on you at any time. The slower pacing of the golden age is gone. We must always factor this in to whatever we do.

Look at the kids of today. How are their interviewing skills?

Do kids talk fast? (from internet speed)

Do kids speak clearly? (from cell phone held to mouth)

Do kids speak in monosyllables and monotone (from texting)

Do kids talk in a staccato manner (from emails)

If habitual behavior can happen to them, how about you? How will you be when presenting yourself? My experience from doing TV commercials can truly help you.

When I made the journey to NYC, my goal was to become a "working actor" on the stage. However, the rent for the next twenty years was paid for from TV commercial residuals. I was cast in the first national commercial that I auditioned for and was cast in most of the others I went up for. I performed principal actor in about forty-five spots, being cast in three out of every four auditions.

To qualify myself in business, here is a list of ad agencies that cast me in their commercials. Actually, I have forgotten a couple and left out the last "Nissan" and two "American Airlines" I did.

Young&Rubicam (5 Nationals) Doyle Dane&Bernbach (3) BBD&O (2) Chiat-day (2) D'Arcy MacManus&Masius (3) Foote Cone & Belding (2) Grey Advertising NW Ayer McCann Ertickson Leo Burnett J.Walter Thompson N. Lee Lacy Scali McCabe & Sloves Stern Monroe Wilson & Griek Daniels & Charles Needham Harper Tempo Advertising Conahay&Lyon Temerlin McClain (5) Macy's Productions Marketing Response Grp (2) Spectrum Assoc. Holderby & Assoc (2) Kitchen Sync Abert Newhoff & Burr

The reason I list these for you is that there are a number of people making up claims of experience. In twenty years, I only had two short periods, when I did not have at least one spot playing on network television. Usually, I had at least two running and one on hold. If you do a bit of basic math, 2 times 20 years, comes out to roughly 40. Which makes my qualification plausible.

Be very careful of who you listen to.

Meanwhile, back to the commercial ranch and how it directly applies to all of you. In spots, I usually played a businessman (for some strange reason a lot of Japanese businessman parts). I also portrayed engineers and professionals. I never got cast as the guy who fixes your toilet. I would have loved to play a "cowboy", but that concept flew even less. I did a good amount of voiceover, such as two years of the entire line of Mazda cars and Bank of America etc. Because of "my look" as they say, I did a ton of print modeling (non-fashion modeling using products for magazines etc.).

But where I can help you most is my experience doing "Spokesperson." This is where you are either the only one in the commercial or the only one speaking to the audience of viewers. Very few actors do spokesperson, because the entire spot rides on one person. Once I was established as a spokesperson, they "play safe" casting me. I become known "in the business."

When you show up on the sound stage to shoot and you are the only one and performance wise it all rests on you, it is very similar to the pressure as a key note speaker or business presenter or pitch in the board room. It is a situation of being given one chance to make it and failure is not an option.

Here is one example for you that sums up experience showing principles of performing under pressure –

In November 1978 or 79, the day before Thanksgiving, I was called in to audition for "a car commercial." I chose wardrobe of a conservative business suit that was in my arsenal of wardrobe that worked for casting auditions. Wardrobe and your "look" are critical in both visual impression and self-confidence. Never wear what your want to wear—always wear the "equipment" that works for you.

I was a favorite actor of the casting director, so I was deliberately scheduled to audition first. The commercial director was one of the most respected in the business. I did what I am teaching you to do –

Connected with him immediately.

Broke the ice with him.

Began a relaxed and trusting relationship with him.

Then I shut up and listened to him with focus.

I then did not do the action of auditioning for them. Instead, I helped them make a decision on what to do with me, even if it means not using me for now.

The director, art directors, and producers, made it clear to me to be available the day after Thanksgiving. I thanked them with my "tag" of a last feeling to leave them with, confirming my confidence and warmth, accepting that we would be working together in two days. The last impression must erase any possible hint of a red flag remaining. It is not over until I am back in my car.

As I exited the audition room, I saw every male Asian actor in Hollywood waiting to go in. I got a couple of "looks of death." It was too late to try to psyche me out.

At 7am sharp, the day after Thanksgiving, I showed up on a Hollywood sound stage at Raleigh studios, which was familiar to me. There was a sparkling polished new car, surrounded by lights and camera. By the bagels, there were two male Japanese-American actors, who were the same age and type as me.

I then got the inside story for this day's shoot. The famous business leader Mr. Lee Iacocca had just become president and C.E.O. of Chrysler Dodge Plymouth, who were now going to announce and introduce to the US the entire line of Mitsubishi cars to be imported from Japan (Colt-Champ-Junior-Arrow-Sapporo etc.—I still remember the copy). Two of the major ad agencies were competing for the new huge advertising campaign. They were told to come up secretly with their best shot and winner would take all. There was a rush as the first spot had to air during the upcoming Super Bowl.

So the ad agency, at this shoot, banked it all on a campaign for the first time in American history, to use a Japanese-American spokesperson to lead the entire major sales introduction of this new line of cars imported to the US. This confidential 911 shoot would both produce the sample pilot to submit to Chrysler Dodge Plymouth and also determine which one of the two ad agencies would get the entire account.

Also to be chosen today on set, would be which one of the three Japanese-American actors would become the Spokesperson for this once in a lifetime job.

How is that for an example of speaking under pressure? Especially, when under the pressure of a 12 hour shoot.

The procedure was that I would be first to both set the rehearsal and lead off the shooting, followed by the other two actors doing what I did. And so we began –

I saw one of the other actors make a deadly mistake of pointing his finger directly into the camera at the viewers. Some are incorrectly coached to do this for emphasis. You point like this if you are shooting your own used car lot local commercial. You do not do this on national television. I actually heard one of the executive decision makers commenting on his pointing,

"He's too pushy."

Be very careful of listening to someone without actual experience. The wrong theory or technique can finish you off.

So for the next twelve hours, I lead off the shoot, focused on doing one thing at a time fully, without the pressure or distraction of only one of us being chosen as the spokesperson.

The next day, my agent called me and said with excitement,

"They want you!"

Sometimes when I was cast, she would say,

"They liked you."

PLEASE NOTE. There is a very important point here. She did not tell me I was the best actor. She did not tell me that my performance was wonderful. The critical point I want you to grasp and accept is in –

"They"

"You"

"Want/Liked"

Is your perspective that you want others to think you are "the best?"

Is your perspective that you want others to think you are "wonderful?" Perhaps your chosen want is harming you.

In truth, it is all about "wanting you."

The Screen Actors Guild, my union, was on the warpath to go on a total strike over TV commercials. They were trying to leverage the holidays and the Super Bowl. Wow! We got the account! Our ad agency won with our spec sample spot and I was to become the first Japanese-American spokesperson on national network television, leading a major ad campaign.

My agent negotiated my high salary, well over six figures, and I was to begin shooting three spots in Japan, three spots in Santa Barbara, and a load of magazine and billboard modeling, plus radio voiceover.

Then, my union, went on strike against TV commercial production. I could not do this incredible gig. The strike dragged on and we ran out of time for shooting my spots for the upcoming Super Bowl.

I was replaced by someone famous who walked on the moon. As I watched the spot on TV, I felt like green cheese being walked on. He even wore the same type suit as me.

As it turns out, a year and a half later, I was cast as spokesperson for Pontiac cars. I was in Detroit, having just finished shooting, and got an impulse to call the ad agency people who ran the campaign I could not do. When I called their number, the receptionist did not at first know who I was calling for. Then she exclaimed,

"Oh yeah. Those are older names. They are no longer here."

"Older names?" The campaign's strike adjusted concept had died out and everybody, from exec to receptionist, got died out too. The big accounts for the biggest ad agencies will cause bloodshed.

Such is life in the pressure cooker.

LESSON LEARNED

You have no competition, only other people auditioning at the same time. If you follow your dream...it is no longer a dream.

The Problem

When I am speaking, with or in front of people, and feel the pressure of an uneasy situation out of my normal comfort zone—

The heart of the problem is,

"I want to be the very best I can be

...but...

I _____."

The "but" creates hesitation, worry, doubt; that not only holds me back from being free, but also can trigger off anxiety from this internal conflict I have created for myself.

The fill in the blank after "I" is the harmful way I look at things, my own incorrect perspective, which can be triggered off by many factors such as –

Being under stress or pressure

Being recorded on-camera

Speaking in front of a group

Meeting face-to-face with a stranger

Interviewing or auditioning etc.

What I then do, my actions, will usually fall prey to my habits, which can consciously or unconsciously be wrong for the results I desire.

EXAMPLE: "I want everyone to be impressed with what I say—but—

I don't know if I will be interesting enough" (so I then push and force from internal conflict).

This is one example in a thousand of a harmful perspectives which trigger incorrect actions, giving me results or consequences I do not want.

Certainly, there are other considerations and many formats while speaking, but if this is not changed, and the heart of the problem is not resolved, then any "technique fixes" are like using bandages on a bleeding artery.

If you change your perspective and your actions, all that is important will follow, because you already have what you are looking for. I will prove this.

The Solution

I help clients who want different results. Whether they are speaking before a business group, leading a meeting, performing on-camera, selling or pitching, interviewing or auditioning, or just meeting with a stranger; clients want significant change in their results. That is all fine and dandy in theory, but there is one real world factor that changes everything.

Time. Our old friend time squeezes us into reality. Many of my clients have a very limited amount of time, which is valuable both personally and professionally. This reality of limited available time, will quickly judge if I provide a solution that really works or if we are just playing with some brilliant sounding hooptedoodle theory.

I do not soften the bite of the word "fee" and change it to "investment." The investment is not the money for the fee. The investment is my client's time. My client is more than capable of making back the money for the fee (or better be if I do my job). But what cannot be made back is their valuable time.

I once heard the founder of a start up company say,

"It is easier to get an audience with the head of some foreign countries, than it is to get a meeting with some C.E.O.'s."

In the real world that I work in, I am fortunate to get a private session with a "C-Executive" for an hour in between returning from Asia and heading for the Ukraine. It is a luxury to get an hour and a half over a delivered lunch. At ninety-one minutes, their executive assistant will be staring at us by the door before I get a bite of my sandwich. If the meeting involves a key note, the speech is not only being written but is held away from the speaker, except in general content, until the writers are finished with it enough to feel safe. Unless you hold office of grand poobah, how can you demand unlimited time to rehearse?

This holds true of most business presentations such as with V.P. of sales and team leader. Everyone in the real world is in a race against time, when everything is on the line. By the time the speech and content are finalized and locked in, it is too late to meet with me. Even best selling authors going out on tour will not have their content set in stone.

I am not complaining. As you can see from my tales, I am used to this. "how ever much time I have—I have, and when it's time to go—it's time to go." This is the reality of it. It is my responsibility to help significantly, given a very limited amount of time. If I do not, I am of no real and practical value to any client.

So I must focus on a genuine key change in the individual's personality—the singer—not the song.

I do not have the luxury of twenty scheduled sessions "on a couch." In one or maybe two sessions at most; what key can we uncover in the person that begins to immediately remove that which holds them back from being the very best they can be. We will succeed, if we focus on the simple solution that works in our real world. Some so called solution that only works in thought, will only add to their anxiety.

I can usually find "the key" in from twenty to thirty minutes. How is this done between phone calls? Every person I meet for the first time, a stranger, is just coming from somewhere, such as an intense phone call or perhaps their child getting ill at school. How do we get anywhere intimate with the personality of a stranger in a few minutes? IF YOU TRY TO USE SOME TECHNIQUE, YOU WILL GET BACK TECHNIQUE. If you try to interrogate or play doctor, you will get back the quality of honesty that all doctors get (who gets lied to more than cops and doctors?). All people have habitual ways of defending themselves with strangers, whether they are effective or not. And this is no time for telling jokes or starting with "We've been having a lot of weather lately." I only know of one way that works within the first twenty minutes. The person must be disarmed. The only way to achieve this is for me to be disarmed. I have to be genuine and open and authentic.

You will see this applied in my true tales within this book.

In some of my tales, such as when undercover, you will see this work under much more dire circumstances than meeting with an executive, where instead of being tossed out and losing my sandwich, I could have become past tense.

If I appear "at ease," it is easier to make the other person feel "at ease." Pretexts and layers of protection must melt. Until temporary trust is achieved, all there will be is surface "yakety -yak." We have to reach the problem and it is always intimate and personal and fragile. But do not blow this up into some kind of psycho-therapy. It is not. It is how to get different results and consequences by identifying and changing our harmful or incorrect way of looking at something that leads us to do different actions, deliberately, by our own choice. It is then impossible for the results to be the same.

My problem with you may be that this all seems too simple for some to believe or have faith in. If this is that simple, then it is do-able. This means the heart of our solution can really work in a very limited amount of time and truly bring change.

I have lived and witnessed it hundreds of times.

The Enemy

Our enemy of helping others is money, power, property, and prestige. If my primary purpose or intention with others is diverted to one of these, I am not helping others—I am helping me. We are now in a relationship of conflict, whether I intend it or not. These harmful desires always get in the way, especially if I covet them and have a strong sense of self-centeredness empowering the delusion of control.

Note. I am not saying to burn your invoice forms and give away all of your property. I am talking about our primary intention in any relationship that should work as a true partnership. This is also not the same as an intimate relationship with someone who you love needing your help. That would be more of an unconditional or natural help. I am talking about a chosen and deliberate intention of helping wholeheartedly.

But if it becomes normal to seek and covet money, power, property, or prestige; then I am set up for our enemy to run the show. I can no longer wholeheartedly have a true intention to help you. I now live in a lie.

I know from experience that if you change from our enemy's normal ways back to what is natural in your heart, you in a moment, right now, can do different actions that will bring you different results with others. Our own worst enemy will melt and become a specific doorway to a new life.

After you pass through into a new life, don't forget to close the door.

Our Perspectives

For our purposes, perspective will mean how we look at things. From an accumulation of how our experiences, thoughts, or beliefs, cause how we see people, places, and things. Some use the terms "Point of View" and others may use "Framing" or "Paradigm."

In this book, I have included a number of what I consider relevant real-life experiences that have shaped my perspective for helping you achieve your needs. As this book is not a biography, I subtracted many experiences from my life to keep on track of our purpose. You must determine selectively and deliberately what perspectives you have that are harming you or holding you back from being the very best you can be in any circumstance.

How do you see what is holding you back? Perhaps not what you are immediately willing to tell me, but what is really holding you back? What is difficult or painful to admit?

You know who is good at this? Children. When kids get honest with you, they almost always know what is wrong. I have seen this in my kid's acting class. It does not mean they will do something different. It just means they know.

With adults, the truth comes harder. Sometimes the initial answer is blame. Sometimes there appears a habit of denial (rationalizing, excusing, justifying, and if none of the above work, start blaming). Sometimes it is truly confusing to the adult. The part of ourselves that we refuse to look at may very well be the part that rules us.

If I first meet you and we begin working to achieve your solution and I start out with this kind of digging, there would be a chance of me being tossed out the nearest window (fight). Or, someone might toss everything on me (freeze). Or, someone might just come up with an "emergency" to suddenly go off to or even "clam up" (run). Are people deep down complicated beings wishing for a simple life? Or are people deep down simple beings who wish they were complicated?

After first meeting a person I am about to help, I must first set this stranger "at ease." Both of us must "disarm." I might begin with,

"What would you like to achieve from our meeting?"

I have never met a human, who had nothing to say, though their reply varies a lot,

"I'm scared to death of doing this."

"I want to be the best."

"I don't know how to do this."

"When I interview or audition, I get all tense."

"I don't like the camera on me."

"Speaking before people is the worst day

"I do a lot of speaking—but something is

I made a business card that reads,

"THE SPEAKER SHRINK"

That always brings a grin. We need to first lighten up a bit or we will just end up in rounds of verbal boxing. A smile is a great start towards intimacy.

Intimacy is our term for what is really going on inside you.

Reminder. If this is too simple, I thank you. I have spent the past thirty-four years of my life making my coaching more and more simple. With people, simple things work, especially under perceived pressure and in the heat of passion.

Is this for just beginners? Advanced work is basics. I don't play golf, tennis, soccer, or marbles. Do basics have anything to do with those? Having almost drowned twice, I can testify that breathing has a great deal to do with swimming.

So whatever a person identifies as what they want, points to what they do not believe or have faith in what they already have. You do not wish for what you already have (too simple?). I now know an important problem in their perspective creating harm to themselves.

I have a great privilege of helping a lot of really smart and brilliant people. I am not their kind of smart and they soon sense that. This gives me an advantage of not being a threat. Many, after a while, want to know about me. These brilliant people are inquisitive by nature. Their curiosity concerning my life can cause,

"We come from very different backgrounds."

ve come from a path of different experiences. My life, as
ou will see from the tales in this book, has not had the structure and sense that their lives have had. Their tremendous
achievements have had a certain logic to them.

Me? My life has been intimately dealing with people, from
the "top of the ladder" to the "bottom of the barrel." Also, I
can honestly say to you that I have never had a primary moti-
vation of money. Clients say that I am "a breath of fresh air." I
do not think that there is anything wrong with a "healthy" person fantasizing about being an actor, a spy, a private eye, a
disco club bartender, a director, a producer/writer, a leader of
soldiers, even a firearms instructor. I sometimes wonder, if
someone actually does all of these things in real life, there has
to be a screw loose somewhere.

So here I sit face-to-face with someone I met twenty minutes ago, working on a change in what is so important now to
both of us. A problem they have lived with.

These solutions that I pass on to you are tried and true. You
already have what you are looking for to make this work. Stop
thinking that you lack or are without. Our answers are already
in our heart and our gut. The problems are between our ears.
These problem perspectives trigger internal conflicts that cause
distractions, keeping us from being the best we can be.

Can be. Not want to be. Those are two very different things.
One is do-able and can always be achieved. The other might
just destroy what we want.

One of the many habitual mistakes I have made in my life
has centered on,

"Another person may not be what I want them to be."

I have violated that principle numerous times and every
time I try to bend it, I get bent. Looking back, if I would have
gotten everything I wanted—I'd likely be dead right now.

How many times have I been wrong with,

"I didn't know."

"I didn't realize that."

and the most common mistake, "Well, I thought –"

So a perspective that is wrong or based on a lie leads to incorrect actions and undesirable results and consequences.

One time I stopped a guy from beating his kid. He wanted to do a better job than his father did. So he thought he was "straightening out his son" but felt horrible about doing so,

"What are you doing?"

"I have to straighten out my son."

"How are you doing that?"

"I hit him with a coat hanger."

"Why are you using a coat hanger on him?

That stopped him cold. His eyes searched for an answer for the first time. Finally, his blank stare moved to me,

"Cause…that's what was used on me."

As far as I know, the coat hanger was only used for clothes from then on.

Don't ever take how we look at things lightly. Perspectives can destroy.

Once I stopped a man from killing his girlfriend. He was obsessing and stalking her and what made things worse was she was egging him on to "control" him. He was driving by her place and secretly feeling the heat of her car engine.

Violence had already reared it's ugly face, when he beat up some poor guy checking her gas meter. It would do no good to ask him,

"How do you feel about that?"

No time for that. When some tough guy, half my age with bloody knuckles stares rage through pink moist eyes, the sand is running out of the timer of real life. Plus, he really wanted to smack somebody and I placed myself close by and convenient. I was convinced that before the sun would go down, he would commit murder. So I began on his terms. Again, begin on the other person's terms,

"You love her so much. You sure you want to kill her?"

It wouldn't work to try to stop him. I needed to support him or we wouldn't get anywhere. The timing was right for this invitation to break and he did. It's times like this that people just need someone to break with.

The key to his perspective was not his girlfriend. She was the dependency. The key was his father. He hated his father's guts. Pure and simple. His violent abusive father destroyed both his mother and his own childhood. His loving mother could take no more and "abandoned" both husband and young son. This was of course devastating for the boy to lose her love. So he made a deep vow to never ever become like his father. I have heard this type of failed vow reverse itself unknowingly so many times. This did not fare well with growing a trust of women.

So I uncrossed my legs and inched my chair back to gain a bit of distance. My arms rested in front of me directly between us. I made ready for the possible incoming fist. Following what I show you in this book, as sincerely and gently as I could, establishing relationship with my feelings and connecting eye-to-eye, I helped this man's pain with,

"What you're doing with your girlfriend… you've become just like your father. What you vowed never to become."

What happened next, I have seen before. The eyes widen a fraction and the pupils register a kind of sudden confusion.

In a moment of complete silence, there is a moment of realization. Not from anything I said, but from a clarity deep within. A lifetime of poison drains away, leaving a new person and peace. My job is to just shut up and be with him at this moment. He finally emotionally exhaled the truth,

"Yes."

That is all he said. That is everything. That is true speaking.

From that moment, this violent man changed. He was not the same. This is the power of a change of perspective. He now no longer wanted any part of his former girlfriend.

Right on cue, the ex-girlfriend got a load of his shocking change, she immediately contacted him and apologized, throwing in wanting to "work things out." We now have another 180 degree turn, but for the wrong motive. When that technique did not pan out, she pulled out all stops to get him to "come over and make up." A classic. When the physical did not work anymore, she panicked. When a controlling manipulator pushes the other person's buttons and they no longer work, there is frantic alarm and panic. This man had a good dose of the truth to ease any of this pain.

The last time I saw this man, he was heading out of the area to begin a new life. I tell you the truth—he had joy and hope. He never did smack me, but he did thank me. I never heard from him again. That is good. Much better than spending his life in prison over a deadly perspective that ruled him.

I once was approached by a former "Enforcer" from the most notorious motorcycle gang in the world. He was just released from I.C.U. for treatment of toxic poisoning. Though he used to harm others and much worse, he truly wanted and worked hard to change his life and by his loving God he was succeeding. I could tell he was afraid of what he might do from his previous way of thinking and doing. He came to me quietly:

"I got a question for you?"

He had my full attention.

"Somebody tried to poison me. When I find out who. I'm gonna' kill them. What would you do?"

I must first listen and pay attention. He did not ask for advice. He was not that kind of man. He meant what he said completely. What would I do? Now is the time one must speak with grace. I intimately confided-

"If you do this…I would absolutely make sure."

The truth is that there was no way of finding who did it. He knew that. He just needed to hear it. The next day he was happier than I have ever seen him. Whenever you touch death and come back living, everything smells different. The truth will set you free.

So I say to you from experience, not theory, that clarity of how you look at something causing you problems is do-able for anyone. You don't have to like it or even agree with it. Most certainly it will not feel normal since you are not used to seeing this truth. The trick is to change this perspective to another that is at least possibly acceptable to you. It is important to realize that if the change is not acceptable to you, it is just an empty wish. Fancy theory does not work in the trenches.

Let's look at and change your perspective so we can change what it causes you to do. Again, it will obviously not be your normal action or what you are used to doing. However, it must be at least somewhat acceptable to you or you simply will not do it (we then end up with great sounding theory or technique that has no practical effect). A human will not continue to do it. If you look at things differently and you then change what you do because of it, the consequences and your results will be changed and different. It is impossible for you to have the same exact results.

This is how you change for real in a brief period of time.

Habits are my Poison

My recruitment into military intelligence was sold to me in the early sixties by the actor Sean Connery. His 007 "Bond, James Bond." got to me in the movie "Dr. No", hooked me in the movie "From Russia With Love" and then polished me off in "Goldfinger." All I needed was a British grey herringbone three-piece suit and a few more inches of height.

It is amazing how movies can affect some of us in our choices in life (and how most of us are taught what we need and lack by advertising agencies).

Secret Agent, James Bond, rescued the world with his looks, charm, and cunning undercover wit. If need be, he took care of villains with his Walther PPK 7.65mm pistol concealed under his left arm. A real spy in the movie world!

But who is a real world spy? The truth is it may be your milk-toast neighbor who mows his boring lawn every Saturday at 9:45am. Or maybe, the lady who sat across from you at the last annual business lunch, or maybe, the board member who is beyond reproach in both scruples and morals. Might they be a secret agent? Naaaahhh. Might they have access to their company's secrets? Might they already have "need to know only" restricted information. Might they have opportunity and access to highly protected areas? Might they be an unsuspected shadow positioned for espionage? Not all espionage is saving the world. Does industrial espionage between businesses exist? What is a non-disclosure agreement for?

In the real world, is it more practical to send in a secret agent or to find some body already in position with "means" and "opportunity?" All you need now for a crime is "Motive."

The main purpose of counter-intelligence is to stop the loss or leaking of information and it is best done to prevent this in its stage of potential motive.

When I was nearing my End of Term of Service date for departing from military intelligence to finally begin my acting career path to NYC, I was called into the office of the commanding officer of the field office. This Commanding Officer (C.O.), was my favorite officer. He was just promoted to Lt. Colonel, having worked his way up in rank, from starting as a private. He was a leader. I once saw him go way out on a limb for one of his men in trouble. His philosophy of leadership favored former President/General Eisenhower because of how much he played golf. He informed me, "If a Leader is working too hard, he's not leading. His ability to delegate well shows in how he spends his time." He sat back and added, "A great leader should know how to do nothing."

Regardless, he was one of only four men I would follow anywhere.

I knew he would cook up some plan to get me to "re-up" and enlist for more years of service. He also knew the chances were slim and none. So he pulled a bunch of strings and came up with an offer to end all offers. He called me in for his one shot and sat me down, smiling his big Irish smile. He took aim,

"How about a little shooter (Irish whiskey)?" He held up a fresh bottle. I went into red alert mode,

"No thank you, Sir. I'm turning over a new leaf."

After his laughter ceased, he set the bottle down between us (maybe some kind of Irish custom). This same C.O. wrote on my official record for promotion that I was one of the "most outstanding individuals" he had ever served with. He also recorded that he would personally appear on my behalf before any board. He knew how to create I.O.U. So off we go,

"I got a special hand picked assignment. Right up your alley."

He lifted up some official looking papers as proof. He interpreted,

"For a six year re-enlistment, you get a five year stabilized tour in Bangkok."

At this time, Bangkok Thailand was the favorite R&R (Rest and Recuperation) destination for soldiers serving in Vietnam. He was offering me the keys to sin city. He searched for weakness in my reaction and then layered the frosting on the cake,

"You'll be undercover plain clothes setting up bar surveillance."

I told you he was good. This would likely be a cover of running prostitutes to find leakage of information in the wicked wild-west saloons of Bangkok. So goes your tax dollars and there was more, "You'll get cost of living allowance, a small villa, and $10,000 cash." An Irish smile let this sink in, followed by, "Tax free, of course."

In 1971, this was a piece of change. With these start-up assets, some clever entrepreneur could reap a big gray area return on investment in the wide-open city of Bangkok.

I actually felt bad turning down the Colonel's hard worked for offer. To this day, I sometimes wonder what may have happened if I took the deal. Of course it would take far less than $10,000 to hire a Thai newsboy to toss a grenade under my undercover bed. We will never know.

I do know that a very disgruntled short-timer agent who came to our field office after a tour in Vietnam jumped at the offer later the same day, after I turned it down. Before that, all he could do was cuss out the army. He even tried to talk me into going in with him in some nutty "Bangkok waterbed scheme" start up.

Meanwhile back at the "motive" ranch. A big part of what we did in counter- intelligence was to investigate military and civilians for top secret security clearances. These were deep background investigations (BI) of people to make sure they had no "motive" or inclination towards falling prey to espionage.

The usual "motive" is blackmail. Your unsuspected neighbor who mows their lawn or your quiet co-worker could be forced to commit the crime by being blackmailed. So we investigate the person, the human, to see if they have weakness in their character that could be exploited to force them to comply with espionage. These are real world spies. Ruthlessly run by "spooks"(spy/handlers who achieve their business goals in any way necessary). This is the dirty end of the stick.

I ran thousands of "leads" in BI cases. I learned a lot about people. The biggest lesson about people is their habits.

Habits are my poison. If you want to ambush me, you first study my habits. If you look for my weaknesses and how to get to me, you study my habits. If you know my habits, you know a lot about my behavior. What I do. How I think. What my usual actions will likely be under pressure, stress, or fear.

Behavior reflects character according to profilers. When you see what someone does in a big time situation, you can determine things about the person themselves. Great clues about a person can come from a deep look at their habits.

Although showing up at your favorite coffee bar at 8:45am sharp every weekday morning to get your fix of the same deep dish latte could be considered habit and a way of ambushing you, for this lesson, we will consider this behavior more towards daily routine,

Our weaknesses and vulnerabilities center more from habitual behavior caused by acquired behavior and accumulated personality. What we are bound to do in fear, danger, during perceived threat or confusion; spontaneously erupted in the heat of passion. We may very well not want to do what we do. We may not even be aware of doing the action. It can just happen. I may even be well versed in my own habits yet still powerless to stop them when the chips are down.

In the top secret investigations, we were more concerned with the stopping of leakage of information before it ever occurred. Our search of a person's character began more with LIDMAC (MI acronym for loyalty, integrity, discretion, morals, and character). How is your LIDMAC? Is it good to go or is it leaning towards derogatory? Are you vulnerable to coercion? Don't blow your LIDMAC!

If you are being "looked into," you have become a "Subject." You will fill out a detailed form of your personal history, from birth to "the present." You will list all places you have lived, all schools, all work, any arrests, etc. Everything. Also listed are former supervisors, co-workers, and listed character references, who will likely say the very best about you.

Because of the workload, your record checks would be conducted by an "old-timer agent" who is no longer up for the footwork of chasing leads. You can learn a lot from these old timers. Such as for those of you who have to frequently change safe combinations and cannot remember the new numbers so well. Just write down on your day calendar to "call fnu lnu (first name unknown last name unknown), or better, any name you choose at phone number such as 408-293-6362. The new combination of your safe is 29-36-3. Now you can get into the company safe without embarrassment. Enough of the spilling of beans.

Meanwhile back at the top secret BI and your LIDMAC showing. An agent would run leads face to face with past and present people starting from your list. If the agent were worth their salt, they would develop character references not listed on your form. People more likely to tell the truth about you. Such as your neighbors and someone not so fond of you. Do you have any of these people in your life? A picture of you will emerge in living color.

A good agent's job is to flush out your true character. You know—the real story. It is also the investigator's job to discern when some rat is trying to slip a dagger in your back. Instincts with people are developed. I, being an over-achiever, was top agent running the most leads monthly for almost two years straight. I assure you, pay more attention to what people do not say.

If you stand up to the scrutiny, you are "good to go"(Army paratrooper slang for ready to jump). However, if your BI starts to head sideways, then your case has turned "Derogatory." You then get promoted to a special investigation and making a "sworn statement" under your best oath. You are a security risk. You are a potential spy ripe for blackmail. You are vulnerable from your habits and behavior.

LESSON LEARNED

Your habits may become your poison.

Our Actions

To act is to do. For our purposes of changing your results, please do not add to, or, complicate this key term. Whether you want to change how you respond with and in front of others, or give a compelling performance on-camera, this is the simple key to achieving your goal. Acting is doing.

How do you look at what you are doing? What are you actively doing as a result of your perspective?

When you are about to make an entrance or stand up to take your turn at speaking, what do you really see yourself doing in your mind? Whenever I question someone about this, no one quite knows what to say.

"What do you mean…what am I doing?"

"Just before you enter or step up…what are you doing?"

Serious people think back seriously,

"I'm going over my content. What I am about to say."

Or they might say,

"I am trying to channel my nervousness."

Or perhaps,

"I am wishing this would be over with" etc.

There could be volumes of replies like these. Some will be chosen, but most will come from habits, either knowing or not knowing that we are doing it. Habitual behavior has a way of taking over in the heat of passion when the "chips are down." Let's just check out these few examples,

"I'm going over my content. What I am about to say."

It may seem natural to justify this self-editing; or is it really habit? Reasons can vary from a desire of achieving "perfection" in those last few moments to "checking that I double-checked to check." I have seen some disturbing themselves because "if I feel too calm something must be wrong." Do we really need this interference just before we enter our situation of perceived pressure.

"I'm trying to channel my nervousness."

Human nerves are like most people, they don't like to be controlled. Are you now focusing on your nervousness? I have heard.

"I think I do better when I am a little nervous."

Or another,

"I usually have a good healthy amount of nervousness."

Really? Would you rather have a chosen focused action that would relieve this nervous state before you begin?

"I'm okay once I get going in it."

I say,

"Okay. But how is your beginning and the first impression of you?"

If you tense your hand and forearm right now, how freely do they respond? If you keep up the tension, in very little time you will start shaking and tiring.

I helped a brilliant person who was given the distinction of representing their company in front of a business audience of hundreds. Up to now, this person's brilliance was achieved drawn into a computer screen forming a habit of channeling "in." Now, for the first time under pressure, they needed to channel "out" to their audience. Many brilliant computer people never signed on for this one. So our brilliant speaker was scared to death, filled with dread and anxiety for the nightmare just ahead. This "stage fright" is intensified by a person who likes to "know the answers" to project into the future. I asked,

"What do you think will happen?"

"I get nauseous, I shake, I am short of breath, I cannot even see clearly; I know I will feel that way."

After I let the misery settle a moment, I leaned into him and drew his eyes to mine, "If I jumped across this table right now, and started to strangle you"…his eyes widened. I then released a smile,

"You would have the very same symptoms. It's called lack of oxygen."

We engaged in a welcome chuckle that opened the gate to reaching his solution. We began to examine his perspective and his actions which fueled his worst fears.

"I'm wishing this would be over with."

Believe it or not, this is one of the most subtle self-lies poisoning the auditions of actors. An audition is basically an intensive job interview. I call this deadly little wish—"showing up to leave." This subtle little thought before entering can cause the appearance of desperation, trying to hard, and wanting to be liked. All of which can unknowingly become the wrong action, especially before you even begin.

With only these three examples of many, you can see how our conscious or subconscious or unconscious action can lead to harmful consequences and results we do not want.

You will read in some of my tales how much people are a subject of habit. When under perceived stress, pressure, or threat; we do what we do.

I'd like to think that I am swifter than all that, so I'll show you how I think I can control all of that. I normally carry my car keys in my right pants pocket, so I decide it would be better to carry those keys in my left pants pocket. Having made the change, whenever I waltz out the front door, I stop to lock it and I have succeeded in changing my door locking life. I can even show off and put those lousy keys back into my pocket and by the time I reach my car, I reach down into my left pocket. I am too cool!

But. The day may come. When you come running up to me screaming!

"There's a bunch of unattractive cannibals chasing me! And! They've got ceramic knives and food processors! Let's get out of here right now!"

My right hand will slam into my right pocket so fast you will only see a blur. Even worse for my coolness will be my screaming,

"Where's my car keys!"

People like you and me are stuck with being human. In the heat of passion, fancy theories fly right out the window. My life has been a study of people. I believe you will actually see that I love people. However, none of us will be hip, slick, and famous, when we appear on the menu for supper.

I side with the military view of "no plan survives contact" or the police view of "you will do how you train" and with a great film actor saying "simpler is better."

Do not ever confuse simple with doing little or nothing. That is incorrect and a harmful perspective.

With us people, simple choices are do-able choices. Do-able choices can be choices that work in the real world. Fancy complicated choices are just so much hooptedoodle.

To act is to do—what are you really doing?…when you get the results you do not want?

The Cornerstone of our Actions

I will now help you with the cornerstone of your solution for anything you wish to do, with and in front of others. In following chapters, I will help you apply our cornerstone to specific formats such as public speaking, business meetings, interviews and auditions, performing on-camera etc. But for now, you can receive this key, for your situation, by the time you finish this chapter. I have no great crown of brilliance for you. I will simply remind you of what you already have. You already have what you are looking for. I understand that there are mechanics to different formats of speaking and I will help you with those needed. First and foremost, we need to begin with the heart of your solutions.

The cornerstone is the foundation. This is the most basic essential and important stone of your structure. If it is solid and works, you will be at ease in what you do. If not, you will always, deep down inside, wonder and worry about its possible collapse. That is not good to help you appear relaxed, at ease, and confident when you are with or in front of other people. Before we begin, there is a deadly warning label. What I give you will be simple and do-able, unless you are unwilling. Prejudice in this case is any negative unfavorable judgment and opinion before the facts are known or even attempted. Please just meet me halfway and this cornerstone will give you the beginning of a new power that can be used immediately in the real world.

Here is an easy probable example of how this works. Most can relate some to the personal difficulties of an actor auditioning for a part. Even if you have never acted, you can envision the stress, pressure, anxiety and difficulty of performing well under an immediate artificial situation. Have any of you ever gone in for a "job interview?" Isn't an actor's audition a type of job interview? Your own job interview can be just as intense and important as an actor auditioning.

Back in about 1999, I was teaching acting full time, with emphasis of on-camera acting and auditioning. The trouble with most acting classes is they focus too much on "acting." If you don't make it through the interview, "you ain't gonna' act." After about twenty years of making a living as a professional actor, I was well acquainted with the possible gut wrenching horrors of waiting to go into the audition. What are you like when you are "Next?" Some of the perspectives can be,

"I don't want to be rejected."

"Please, please let them like me."

"Everything is on the line for this job."

"What if they don't like me?"

"If I don't get this—I'm finished."

"What if they like me…but?" etc.

We could fill an encyclopedia with these types of fear issues.

Based on my observations of acting professionally for over twenty years and teaching it for over thirty-four years, most people lose the job before the audition or interview begins. If you are not an actor, an audition is a job interview.

The head begins to run. The actor auditioning with a script can go off with the wrong actions (doing the wrong things).

"I'll show them how great this can be done."

"I'll make bold choices that no one else will make. (I actually heard this being "taught"). My question is simple, "how do you know what choice others have made?"

"I will be better than anyone else."

Again, we have an encyclopedia of wrong choices that are great fuel for the fire of anxiety.

Those experienced in casting, producers, directors, will privately tell you that most actors "come in" too desperate, trying too hard, and seeking to be liked. Just like any other intensive job interview. Those who are searching for the right person to do the job are looking for "the singer" they already have "the song."

So in 1999, I began this life changing conversation,

I begin with, "When you audition (or job interviewing), what are you doing?"

The job seeker is confused,

"What? What do you mean what am I DOING? I'm auditioning for the part."

I clarify, "A job acting?"

"Yeah. I want the job."

"I understand you are auditioning, that is the general reason communicated. But, instead, I ask you "What are you really doing? How do you look at it personally?"

"Well…I see an audition as_____(fill in the blank with an issue) So I am getting the job by _____(fill in the blank with habitual behavior)."

It is now time to throw them out of their box. I ask them or you,

"Would you HELP someone you care about?"

The look in the eyes is not knowing what is happening. It draws out,

"Yeahhhh. Of course."

"You look like a nice person. Do you like helping someone you care about?"

"Sure. I like helping people…I care about."

"It feels good."

"Yes, it does."

I then lean my eyes a few inches toward their eyes,

"Then I want you to stop auditioning. Do not ever audition anymore."

Now they are empty. Disrupted. Even talkative people have nothing to say,

"I want you to do this action instead of auditioning. I want you to help others make a decision on what to do with you… even if it means not using you right now." Wholeheartedly.

I heard a group of actors from England's Royal Shakespeare Company refer to this as "intention." This is an essential part of really good acting. The question becomes "What is your intention?" "What are you doing?" Is your intention to?

Win others over

Take charge

Get others to give you what you want

Manipulate others

Control etc.

If we throw whatever intention you may think you have out the window right now, and focus authentically on helping others in your heart, you will immediately;

Feel differently

Look differently

Smell differently

And react and respond differently

If you just simply help others, you will no longer have that desperate feeling of going after others. Instead, you will have a secure comfort and ease, drawing others to you instead of chasing them. You already have the ability to do this. You do not have to study. You have your own life's experiences.

"Make a decision, " in this cornerstone, it is not being wishy-washy or passive. This is being active and decisively taking risk. Making a decision is decisive. The decision maker takes action. "Controlling others" is a delusion. If I help others to make a decision, I then have the power to influence.

"On what to do with me." How many lose the job because they unknowingly intrude upon the decision maker's job. For an actor, it is more important to be able to follow direction than it is to act. If you do not seem to be able to follow direction, you "ain't gonna' act." Can you just simply listen and do? There is the person you want for the job.

Are you assuming that the decision makers know what will happen months from now? Do they have a magic crystal fortune-telling ball? Most decision makers know that no one knows what will happen, but when it does happen, you want someone who can deal with it, and make things work with what they have.

The final phase is critical but not popular, "Even if it means not using me right now." Do not help with strings attached. If you take this to heart, you are no longer owned by whom you are dealing with. You are free! When you are free, you become much more attractive. This may be hard, but it sure is powerful. Besides, have you not gotten something later from business? If you are remembered, has something come to you later? Instead of getting everything now, how about just making the meeting worthwhile.

When going up for a job, how do you know that it is still open? The audition or interview itself may be used to simply make a decision on what to do with you. If you lined up all the actors, who make a living at it, and told them,

"All of you professional experienced actors who have been cast in a part that you were not originally called in to read for —take a step forward."

The entire line of experienced actors would step forward. No one would be left behind. If you then told this seasoned line of actors,

"All of you actors in line who have been cast in a part you never even read for—take another step forward."

The entire line of pros would step forward. Decision makers are looking for the singer—they already have the song.

If any decision maker has already thought about the job, it is only human to visualize someone in their own mind's eye. What are the odds that you are exactly what they visualized? More so, what if there are more than one decision maker? Now you have multiple pre-conceived images of "the right person" for the job. Even if someone says, "I will remain completely open for the hiring." It is not possible to prepare for hiring with a total blank mind.

So it's all about you deliberately influencing others and getting them on the same page. Your page. This begins from first impression, before you even say a word, and goes on to last impression, as you exit.

For auditions, interviews, sales, pitching, etc. "I'm going to help others make a decision on what to do with me, even if it means not using me right now."

Or for meetings, presentations, speeches, etc., "I'm going to help you make a decision." Or just simply, "I'm going to help you." This is done wholeheartedly.

If you are skeptical that this can work for you in the real world, millions of people who were hopelessly addicted to alcohol or meth or heroine or whatever; have been freed from that bondage by helping others. How hopeless is your problem compared to theirs?

I tell you the truth. It really works. It is proven every day.

CHANGING YOUR OUTSIDE
From Rock 'n' Roll to Lock 'n' Load

In the section, "Recovery Is Getting Back Something I Lost," I will deeply go into my childhood. Let's begin here with the approach of Willow Glen High School graduation class of 66'.

After my father came down with terminal cancer and I had a mother and two younger sisters to consider, I traded in my dreams of becoming an actor for the job stability of law enforcement. Truthfully, I would have made a lousy cop. But I made a good soldier.

At the state college, during the 1960's, which was over-crowded from those avoiding the draft, I was awarded, in the first year of military Reserve Officer's Training Corps (R.O.T.C.), the Distinguished Military Student Medal. Only one cadet was awarded this medal in each of the four yearly levels. It was rumored that the cadet awarded this could lead to a regular army commission (not reserve but the same type of commission as West Point).

In the 60's, this country was torn wide apart. Even the rock 'n' roll was split up between James Brown Motown, Liverpool's Beatles, and California surfing. Hippies introduced a new dress code and draft cards and bras became fuel for illegal bon-fires. It would take an encyclopedia to fill in the blanks from this incredible decade of turmoil.

By the rebellious year of 1968, I was sick of state college. My father was in remission of cancer and my family seemed to be doing okay. The first love of my life had just married another man so I was ripe to join the French Foreign Legion.

At that time, I did not like to be told what to do, so I joined the Army. This enlistment occurred after the deadly TET (Vietnamese New Year) Offensive of 1968 Vietnam. My attitude at the time was—"If I'm going to die, I may as well get it over with. If I survive, I will use my GI Bill to study acting in NYC. If I don't survive, my GI insurance will go to my family."

I signed up for an extra year of serving to become a counter-intelligence agent for military intelligence. It became time to get ready to report for duty.

At the Induction Center, in the worst area of Oakland, California, we were all put up eight to a room in "the roach hotel." Half the guys were let out of "juvi" (juvenile hall jail) with a generous choice of future, "Go into the army or go to prison." Acceptance is easy if you have no choice.

The night before our physical exam, we drew cards. I drew a bed with a young pool hustler named LeRoy. LeRoy and I then flipped a coin for which one of us would sleep under the sheet and which one on top. This turned out to be futile as in the middle of the night we were awakened by the sound of a handgun butt pounding on our hotel door. There was much colorful language echoing in the hall of the roach hotel.

It seems that some guy, temporarily released from juvi, had taken advantage of his new found freedom. He engaged the services of a street prostitute and then neglected to pay for his services. Her enraged talent agent was now at our door with a gun, swearing vengeance. We yelled through the door that he had the wrong room and to go search somewhere else for a punk with a grin on his face.

The pounding moved down the hall. We were now wide-awake from other than a bugle, so we spent the remaining few hours telling lies to each other.

The highlight of the army induction center physical the next morning had to have been when about forty of us were directed to form a circle in a large room. A very distant look-ing man in a crumpled white lab coat stood in the middle of this circle. He then gave the order,

"Turn around and face the wall!"

We did so in an almost soldierly manner. He then gave firm instructions,

"Now. Drop your pants."

A moment of silence was followed by hesitant inactivity. He continued,

"I said drop your pants! Underpants too."

Forty complexions became ruddy. The circle dropped skivvies prompting,

"Now. Bend over"

Forty heads turned. I noticed the young punk out of "juvi," who burned the street walker, developed a strange smile on his face.

As the circle of men bent over, I recalled that the Japanese believe this same position, looking back through one's legs at Mt. Fuji, will bring them good luck. I don't know about that, but I looked backwards, from under, at the circle of men bent over and was certainly given a majestic view. We all were loudly reminded,

"Bend over and look at the wall in front of you." As if we would head for a parade. Then came the coup de grace,

"Now spread your cheeks!"

As I processed the possible meanings of this last instruction, I noticed the guy bent over next to me beginning to reach for his face. We heard loud and clear clarification from the voice of authority,

"No! No! Your butt!"

This must be some military synonym, like a gentlemanly way of expressing "get off your cheeks."

With a great lack of willingness, we all followed orders. Orders are orders. I spied on the man in the lab coat. In the middle of our circle, he turned slowly in a counter-clockwise manner until he completed one revolution of binary angles. After his thorough medical examination was completed,

"Stand up straight and pull up your pants."

Apparently, we all had whatever it was he was looking for. He declared,

"You're all good. You passed."

How nice it is to be diagnosed as healthy. The remainder of the army physical was just as thorough and thoughtful. You would have to be quite dead to not pass.

We were separated into groups. Being the eldest at twenty years and eleven months, I was placed in charge of leading the inductees to San Francisco airport. We would catch a plane for Seattle/Tacoma airport (SEATAC) and then board a bus to Fort Lewis, Washington. I also was placed in charge of the group's paperwork. I took charge of leading the seventeen to eighteen year olds.

I had my first deserter at the first railroad crossing we came to. Our bus slowed approaching the railroad tracks and then stopped according to the law. One of the guys jumped out of the bus window head first. He landed and took off running down the railroad tracks. The last I saw him, he was heading south towards the direction of Mexico.

United Airlines flew us towards SEATAC airport in Washington state. The airlines also supplied us with gorgeous "stewardesses" in 60's short skirts. The air cabin pressure rose from teenage testosterone. Free from drinking age laws at 20,000 feet, the cabin bar was open to anyone. It is amazing how mini bottles, when chug-a-lugged by teen guys, can boost bravado.

After the gorgeous stewardesses finished torturing us and waved good luck, we were quickly trapped into an old bus heading south to our destination. It is further amazing how many front seat shenanigans of couples driving below the high bus windows can be spotted by fifty guys heading towards their doom.

Rueben Maria Ramirez, a "pachuco (zoot suit gang)" descendant from El Paso, was very busy in the back of the bus smoking up his entire bag of "mary jane." He had a new gang of newfound friends.

We arrived at Fort Lewis in drizzling rain, missing dinner, with a pack of teenagers "stoned out of their gourds."

So it was fitting that the first stop is the amnesty hall. Our disabled group of forty-nine out of fifty joined other groups in the large room. We all sat in silence. Something was up.

A sergeant took charge of the large room and informed us in no uncertain terms, that anything illegal or even barely legal was to be surrendered immediately and placed on the big table next to him. He assured all, "No matter what you give up—if you put it on that table right now—you are guaranteed full immunity from prosecution. That means that nothing you give up will be held against you."

Some of the faces sank. The sergeant continued while he pointed to four military police standing nearby, who looked like they just sucked on a lemon.

"But! If you hold out anything. Anything at all! When we search you –"

Everyone squirmed as he pushed on,

"You will get busted. Jail. Court Martial. Maybe the firing squad.

Now! Put all your _ _ _ _ on the table. Now!"

Rueben Ramirez, from vast experience facing authority in El Paso, led the way of surrender. He strut up in grand jail style and stared at the sergeant with a grin. Rueben flung a remaining bag of marijuana onto the table. Ceremoniously, in his flannel shirt, only buttoned at the top; from his upper left tee shirt sleeve, he untwisted a concealed switchblade knife. Out of either, nostalgia or safety, Rueben pushed the little button and flipped out the blade one last time. He tossed his trusted compañero onto the table and dusted his hands signaling childlike "all done." He then tried to locate his seat and what direction he had come from.

The army's pillage on the tables was impressive. At this time, there was no airline security like today. "No guns. No knives. No mace." There were piles of liquor, drugs, knives, and pistols (Surprised? We were entering the army right?).

Many look back on army basic training with repulsion and waste. I look back on it as one of the finest lessons in people anyone could ever experience, because all individuality was stripped away in days. All that remained was people.

The next morning we were sent to "reception" or what was quaintly called "Casual Company." We were again in a big old wood hall. Another sergeant ordered,

"On your feet!"

We all stood up with stiffness. He did his routine,

"We need to find some special men. If you never finished the sixth grade—sit down." Some teens took their seat with disappointment. He continued,

"If you never got out of junior high eighth grade—sit down." More sat.

"If you never graduated from high school—sit down now."

A surprising number took their seats. A large part of the room was seated.

"If you never finished the first year of college—sit down."

Now all but a handful were seated.

"If you never graduated from college—sit down."

I took my seat with regret. The seated group narrowed their eyes and grit their teeth staring at the few still standing. Those still standing started to grow a smirk on their face. The sergeant announced as a reward,

"All of you standing are college graduates—right?"

Their heads nodded in affirmation. The sergeant changed tone of his voice,

"We are putting you college graduates in charge of...passing out the pencils."

A roar of laughter shook the old wooden hall. Even guys who could barely write their name had a huge horse laugh. The college graduates had a long walk to the front to fetch the pencils.

Basic training has only eight weeks to convert a mess of boys into a unit of men, working together as a team.

The upper part of our individuality was lost in the famous barber chair. Think about how important "the hair" is to individuality.

I was seated waiting for my turn in the barber chair. These army barbers had the amazing ability to shave off all of your hair with only a few strokes of an electric razor. My now compadre, Rueben Maria Ramirez, was waiting for his cut and the end of his huge 60's pompadour slick backed curly hair. Only two passes of the electric razor made it through the top of Rueben's head. All of the greasy pomade hopelessly jammed the razor. As the barber cursed and attempted to clear his razor, I looked up and saw the bald path on the top of his head and the two remaining puffs of black hair on each side. With his large pursed lips, he looked like some kind of Mexican Mickey Mouse. Rather than being a gangster in El Paso, he now looked like he could blow up balloons at children's birthday parties in Juarez. I cracked up over this and got into a bit of trouble before my turn at hair styling.

When everybody dresses the same way, eats the same, use the same latrine, and has no hair, you really learn that all men are the same. Every man is equal and has the same needs and feelings. You hear this all the time in fancy speeches, but it becomes real when you live with fifty men in the barracks and your identity is 2nd Platoon, Charlie Company, 4th Battalion, 1st Brigade (Chargin' Charlie C-4-1).

The youngest man in Charlie Company was recruit private Corky, who weighed in at fourteen years old. He had a baby face, rosy cheeks, and was a bit late in change of voice. The drill sergeants had fun sport teasing private Corky while he stood rigid at "attention" and squeaked,

"Yes sir drill sergeant!"

The sergeants would then threaten to transfer him to the girl scouts.

Young Corky volunteered for "this man's army" after wearing out his welcome at reform school. It seems in a fit, he hit his female English teacher on the head with the nearest schoolroom chair. He lied about his age to the army recruiter (easy in 1968) and was welcomed into the sea of olive drab uniforms. The recruiter paid back the lie with a lie and fished Corky into enlisting for an extra year to go to "medical school" and maybe prepare for becoming a doctor at Fort Sam Houston, Texas. The naïve fourteen year old in reality signed on to become a "combat medic."

While we were receiving our shots from "short-timers (draftees just returned from Vietnam and finishing out their last few months by counting their days). The attitude of short-timers can best be described as from bad to worse. Three of them were giving our line of recruits multiple shots with a gun that blasted numerous serums right through the skin and into the arm. Shoot left arm-move up-right arm-move up- left arm again-move out.

These three medical shot shooters vented their rebellious attitudes by dancing to rock n' roll music in place and shooting us in the arm at significant lyrics of the song from the boom box. Between shots for laughs, they had target practice shooting serum at lined up paper cups. My left arm received medical malpractice when the shot shooter missed and glanced the ultra high powered serums across my upper arm, instead of directly into it. Like being shot with a bullet, my upper left arm was sliced open from the stream of the shot. I bled a lot. So good, that the jerk that shot me grimaced and advised,

"You better get that looked at; but stay in line for now."

The drill sergeants saw my arm and enjoyed a quiet laugh over the bloodshed. Private Corky, who enlisted unknowingly to become a combat medic, stood behind me in line. When the fourteen year old saw my arm, he began to faint at the sight of my blood. Not good for career potential as a medic.

Ruthless for number quotas were the army recruiters in the 60's. One poor disappointed kid learned that he would not learn a valuable trade in "aerial surveillance," instead, he had volunteered for an extra year to become a door gunner on a helicopter.

Each platoon was led in basic by a drill sergeant "lifer," sporting a "Smokey the Bear" hat and a pocket emblem that read "This We'll Defend." One of the great fortunes of my life was my 2nd Platoon being assigned a Drill Sergeant who was the most decorated soldier on post. Our Drill Sergeant was a tall very lean Texan with steel blue eyes, under his Smokey hat. He spoke with a drawl from under his small neatly cropped handlebar mustache. Years before, when he was seventeen years old and serving in the Korean war, he was awarded for gallantry in combat the Distinguished Service Cross. The only higher medal for valor in combat is the Congressional Medal of Honor, which was the only medal he did not have. This sergeant of two wars was decorated with twenty-seven medals for valor under fire. Included were nine Purple Hearts for wounds received in combat. He joked to me,

"Ah git hit evrytahm ah go out."

This was followed by a satisfied chuckle. He then told me how he was so lean, from his last recovery,

"Ah wuz with th'Americal Division. An we got hit one night. charlie (VC = Victor Charlie) charged us. Some dink set off a clamore mine off a hisself (explodes steel balls shooting out). Took out our whole section n' the boy next ta' me got killed. Ah got hit too n' knocked down ta' the bottom a' the hole we wuz in. Had a 12 gauge shotgun layin' at the bottom a' the hole an' sum how ah got back up enough to level the shotgun on top a' that foxhole. That damn charlie was still try-ing ta' crawl at us with his guts blown out. He pulled a satchel charge with him."

That same satisfied smile returned to his handlebar mus-tache,

"He wuz sure surprised ta' see my shotgun barrel in his face. I blew his head clean off...thin passed out. So they sent me home ta' die—but here ah am agin."

The Texan who was about 34 years old and looked 54, shook his head,

"Sure 'nuf. Evrytahm ah' go out—ah' git hit."

The day before our first day on the rifle range, the platoon gathered before our drill sergeant in the lower barracks. Care-fully, he checked outside the windows, to make sure, the coast was clear. He addressed the entire platoon,

"At ease n' listen up."

A father like tone brought on everyone's full attention,

"Tamarrah ya'll gonna have rifles an' live ammo. Any buddy got a grudge on me—an' figures puttin' a round in me—think 'bout this…"

The salty sergeant unbuttoned his lower shirt.

"Ah alwuz get a gun on me. Ya'll maybe don' see it …"

Drill sergeant removed a Colt Python 357 magnum with a short 2½ inch barrel, from under his olive drab fatigue shirt. There is one clear purpose for this concealed gun. He reassured us in a gentle calm manner,

"Ah bin killin' min since ah wuz sevteen. An' 'nother one 'er two—ain' gonna' make much diff'rence." His handlebar mustache broke into a friendly grin.

This is compelling speaking that is crystal clear. All fifty-two members of 2nd platoon needed no further clarification in this presentation. Team leadership.

Soon, Drill Sergeant made me a trainee squad leader. Soon after that, I was made trainee in charge of the entire Company C and it's one hundred fifty young men. Under me in leadership, each of the three platoons had a platoon guide over four squad leaders. Beneath the cadre, I led the company.

The code of the infantry is "FOLLOW ME!" I believe this simple code is a fundamental business lesson to all who lead, especially under pressure or danger. I would follow our drill sergeant anywhere. I can say that about very few others.

Stripped of all pretense and individuality, this unit of men would teach me invaluable lessons about how to realistically lead and how we react to power, threat, and fear. A squad is a unit within a platoon that consists of eight to twelve men (not unlike how many business's structure their teams, as there is a limit to the number that can effectively function as a single unit). Numerous men were tried out to be squad leaders. Most were fired and replaced. Why? It begins with the perspective of a leader or one in charge.

Most of these young men would tell you that a leader "tells everybody what to do." This perspective may have come from parents, teachers, or police. So what do these young men do to lead their squad? They do habitual behavior from their own short path of experience. They do "threaten like police, make you do like their teachers, or do yelling like they got at home." That is why so many could not last as squad leaders. Most people do what was done to them.

There are at least two ways to get someone to clean the toilets. The better way is not ordering them to do it. It is best to want to do a good job, in fairness and for the good of the entire squad, of which all are a valuable part of. Then the toilets will not be just clean, they will shine. I witnessed this.

I have heard it said that most people would like to be in charge. I no longer believe this. I think most people like to fantasize about being in charge. However, when some threat kicks in the door and screams "Who is responsible for this!" Most people would rather reply very quickly,

"Talk to my boss."

When someone responds to this door explosion by standing and owning,

"I am responsible." Here is your leader

Power is a key to people. It is at the core of the deepest button in any addiction and at the core of the heart of a great leader. Our battles may be over symptoms but the long war is over power.

To be honest with you, I would not have guessed that the condensed form of this chapter would be half this long. This tells me that almost fifty years later, I still do not fully grasp how much this period of my life impacted me today. That war was fought a lot by teenagers and early twenties, who had neither the money nor the resources to avoid serving. Many seventeen year-old drop outs showed up newly engaged to be married or with a fresh tattoo. It was an era when nobody said to us, "Thank you for your service."

To this day, I have not visited "The Wall." It is not so much The Wall. It is the names on The Wall. When we graduated from basic training, we all walked away in different directions.

But the night before, I had charge of the company and managed to lead our troops into smuggling into the barracks a load of soda, smokes, playboy magazines, and enough beer to get a buzz on without starting a riot.

During the entire period of basic training, I managed not to get fired as the trainee company leader. I was not challenged to get into the boxing ring from resentment. No one shot at me (though I think I know who shot at our lieutenant).

Instead, I got the entire company to practice extra drill on their Sunday late afternoon off. Part of this was from my bribing a disaffected corporal, with no real authority, to verbally okay my marching the platoons, one at a time, across the street to the off-limits snack shop. I stuck my own neck out to bring all of the men to a feast of forbidden pizza and sodas. Somehow I managed to keep order, even present with the flirting teen girl who was heating the pre-made little pizzas.

It is amazing how far people will follow you when they see you stick your own neck out for them.

The Captain kept trying to get me to go to officer candidate school. He finally settled on giving me the award of –

Dennis K. Sakamoto "Outstanding Trainee" C – 4 – 1

I still have that little statuette of an Infantryman waving his hand high in the air with the inscription 'FOLLOW ME!" This is a true way to lead others.

I still keep some snapshots of this bunch of young men having our farewell party with a bunch of shaved heads and goofy smiles. There is a memory of private Corky talking to his mother after our graduation ceremony. The fourteen year-old only son, glowing, as he lied to his visiting mother about how great this all is and how he looked forward to medical training. But what I remember most was his mother; her feigned smile and the moist worry in her eyes.

LESSON LEARNED

M/F—FAMILY—CULTURE—ENVIRONMENT—BIRTH
ORDER—GETS US EVERY TIME

Here lies a critical fundamental chapter of the greatest importance and only you hold the answers.

Where do your perspectives come from? How did you form, "how you look at things?" What caused you to see things as you see them? There are many possible influences but the main ones are:

Male/Female

Family

Birth Order

Culture

Environment

We were born into the first four with no choice of our own. Environment, what we are surrounded by later in life, can be by choice, such as where we work.

This is all so obvious. Maybe too obvious. Once again, many times we lose things in the most obvious places.

These five influences are often woven together in combinations. Culture may be less influence to someone who has family roots here for 300 years, as opposed to a person who just immigrated here. But all five influences are fundamentally within us and we are all whole. Look first within these and you will usually find the roots and key to the problem.

If you and I met privately to seek the key to a perspective that is holding you back, the first place I would look is when you were in your teens or younger. Certainly, this is not always the case. Also, obviously you have evolved with time. Recent environment could have deeply affected this.

Please know that my purpose is not to "psycho-analyze" (which I am not qualified to do). My purpose is to help someone find their own key to any harmful perspective, usually within a few hours. So far, this can and does happen.

The answers are yours. Everyone has their own unique path of life's experiences. But once you have the key, you have the solution.

At this point, let's look at fear. Here is a proven way to uncover it.

First, get a piece of paper and a pencil. Please not a computer.

Next, write down your problem. You have an idea of what it is.

Then, from this problem, write down what you are afraid of.

Once you admit to and write down what you are afraid of, treat that as "on the surface." Then write down the truth of "what are you really afraid of?" This will be short and very personal. It will not contain other people, places, or things; as was likely in the previous listed surface fear. It will be painful and hard to admit. It will usually contain the word "I" or "me."

Having admitted this deeper fear on paper, reflect deeply on where it came from. You will know. It came from somewhere in the past. Where or from who?"

When you identify and uncover this harmful perspective that is not working for you, come to a decision. Do you really want to maintain this way of looking at things? If so, keep doing what you are doing and you will keep getting what you are getting. If not, what is a change in your perspective, that is acceptable to you, to commit to from now on. That "acceptable to you" is important because it makes the solution do-able. If your change is not acceptable to you, it will not work in the real world. It is a nice sounding thought that you will not do. You don't have to like it, you just need to go along with it. If it was attractive to you, you would have done it a long time ago. Acceptance will come from doing.

The influence of "issues" of male/female, family, birth order, culture, environment, are written in concrete. But that does not mean they have to rule us. I have personally witnessed thousands of people, as in human, being freed from this bondage of self.

If you examine your life, there are numerous things that you once believed but no longer believe. You have the potential for turning around one hundred eighty degrees in one brief moment of clarity.

LESSON LEARNED

If there is a part of ourselves that we refuse to look at, that part will rule us—no matter how long ago it was.

Everyone Has an Accent

Everyone who speaks has an accent. Some call this a dialect. Usually a dialect refers to a manner of speaking within the regions of a language, such as American Southern, or American New York City. We generally use accent for referring to a foreign manner of speaking our own language. For our purposes, I will just use the term accents for all manners of speaking.

An accent is how someone forms the talking sounds of vowels and consonants. Wherever a person is from, they have become used to speaking in a distinctive way. The lilt or rhythm of speaking is normal to the area and when speaking in a non-native area, the speaking sounds different. Like I emphasize a perspective change in this book—there is no right—there is no wrong—just different. I am not referring to morals. This perspective can remove distractions.

An accent can carry over a music and personality from its origin. It can also hold traits of the person's original root language and culture. Everyone has an accent. If you do not think you have an accent, just move far away. You will be crowned with one.

In the army, guys usually hung with guys from their same area of origin. They had close to the same accents. Charlie from "Hutlanna Gawjah" hung with Dwight from "Sou Calannah weh hiz Dahdee wuzfum." The guys from "Nu Yaawk" kept together. The guys from California usually mixed with everybody. One guy from Peabody Kansas wanted no part of anybody.

I actually was under the misconception that being from California, I did not have any accent. I was set straight by a lifetime dedicated speech teacher, when I started out acting in NYC. I then worked hard to develop my speech to what American theatre calls "Standard English."

By the way, here is a very important warning label—never try to correct your speech while performing or doing your presentation, meeting, interview, audition, etc. You will come across as disconnected and in your own head. Correct your speech on your own, outside of your business. I made this critical error in the beginning of my acting career.

After I developed speaking in Standard English as a habit, I was hired by Academy Award winner Jose Ferrer. His diction and enunciation was legendary, as witnessed by his award winning verse as Cyrano de Bergerac. After meeting with Mr. Ferrer, he informed me,

"You speak well."

This was a treasured compliment for me. However, that was when he auditioned me on Thanksgiving morning 1975 at his 57th street apartment.

Now, after over twenty years of doing over forty-five TV commercials, my speech headed toward the laundromat. You cannot be cast as an American in a fast food commercial speaking in Standard English. You are better off with,

"Yummee! I gotta' git more a' this!"

As would have it, I had to do a lot of Asian accents on television. Training hard in Standard English, I got paid for doing Japanese, Chinese, Korean, Vietnamese, etc. I dedicated two years correcting my speech so that I could get paid messing it up worse.

This leads us to a key lesson for you and your accent. When I did many accents both on-camera and voiceover recordings, the major concern was –

"Who is your audience?"

I was doing the accent for the American audience, not for the audience of the accent. Therefore—accuracy of my accent was not the most important thing—being understood was what was the most important to my employer.

So my accents were directed to be watered down and adjusted for fear of the American audience giving up trying to understand me. That is what happens with an audience—if the audience cannot understand you—they will give up trying to understand you.

Go to a restaurant of foreign food. Find a worker who can barely speak English. They without doubt have an authentic accent. Now try to talk with them. The conversation will be brief for both. Both of you will give up. It is useless.

Just because your audience has not walked out on you, does not mean they haven't given up on you. Especially with cell phones and tablets, are they taking notes or are they really doing something else instead of listening to you?

"But I don't speak any foreign language!"

Okay. But does your environment cause you to work at today's pace? If so, have you developed from your work or lifestyle the following accent?

"Fast!"

Do you have a "fast accent" when speaking? Do you speak at the speed of a text or email? Do you project your voice beyond the distance of a cell phone receiver to your mouth? Do you talk too fast? That is also an accent.

Since the onset of the internet, I have heard a progressive nose dive in clarity of speaking. If you do not believe me, talk to your kids. How about some teens?

The young now mumble in short staccato sounds resembling the grammar of a text or email, without feeling, expression, or detail. How goes your family discussion over the dinner table?

You, "How was your day?"

Kid, "Fin."

You, "Well, what did you do?"

Kid, "Nothin."

I now have hearing loss from gunfire and loud bars. Maybe my hearing loss has made me seem like a better listener. But many now talk as if the other person's ear was next to their mouth like a cell phone.

Everything is drawing us inward, like towards a small screen. We are losing projecting ourselves outward.

In Silicon Valley, the environment is fast and busy. I have worked with numerous clients with accents from India, China, and Germany. With actors, I have worked with the most common accent of Spanish. All of these accents can share a deadly consequence when speaking American –

They talk too FAST. Especially, in the heat of passion caused by excitement, enthusiasm, and pushing to get the point across. But if they are concerned about their accent, speeding up can be a result that makes understanding more difficult.

I guess it is about time for a solution that works for foreign and fast accents. This solution is already within you and you already know how to do it.

You are reading this book in English from left to right. You go from one word to the next left to right. This is how we learned English and it is now habitual behavior while doing. When we write, we follow the same manner.

However, when we speak, we do not speak from right to left, one word at a time. That is to say –

"We – should – not – speak – like – this."

When anyone speaks, communicating clearly in any language, we do it in thoughts and phrases. Such as:

"Yesterday morning – I went to the market – to get some fruit."

Thoughts and phrases for a smooth natural flow with clarity.

If I literally speak what was written in a linear manner, word by word, I will go into a monotone. Boring. Knowing that is not acceptable, the accent I speak with will now make understanding me harder when I try harder to emphasize. What happens if I am distracted, by being informed, "they have a hard time understanding you." I become a victim of habit.

The habit most common for driven people is to do it harder to overcome. Now communication can be harmed further.

The importance of the content will lead the listener to frustration because it feels like it is being missed. People give up pretty easily. How much patience has the internet fostered and developed?

Here is an example of how I clarify what thoughts and phrases are in just a few minutes. In this instance, with an Indian C.E.O./PhD, who did not mind my corny way of getting directly to the point. I kicked it off with,

"I really like Indian food."

"Of course. So do I."

"What is your favorite dish?"

"But you have never heard of it."

(That is PhD talk. So I counter with Private Eye talk)

"Try me."

He then names an Indian dish that is a mouthful. Fill in the blank,

" _____ "

"How do you make this wonderful dish?"

"By making a reservation at a proper Indian restaurant."

"Please help me to understand. How would you make this dish?"

The executive nods and leans towards me, checking if I am listening,

"First…."

"Yes. Go on."

"You get the proper ingredients."

I am listening intently. The C.E.O. continues,

"From a good quality Indian market…"

This speaker is now focused on my absorption of all content he is presenting me, rather than his accent. Seeing that it is important to me, he does not do this fast, but speaks at a natural pace based on my receiving his content.

"Make sure you get garam masala."

In less than one hour, we have made this brilliant speaker understandable, even with his Indian accent. He will no longer speak in a linear fashion, word by word, like he learned to read English. He will communicate in thoughts and phrases, allowing his audience to receive his content and the points being made. You cannot do this if you speak with a "fast accent," like many American speakers.

Remember this. The pace or speed by which you speak effectively is not determined by the speaker. It is determined by your audience or listener. Whether that be one person, or a thousand receiving your message.

If a speaker has a foreign accent, and they get their message across clearly, I believe they become much more interesting speaking with their accent. They can appeal to an audience with their unique foreign charm. What was considered a shortcoming can be turned into an advantage with the change of perspective and action of –

"Helping others to make a decision on what to do, by helping them to truly understand communicating through thoughts and phrases."

The only time this has backfired on me was with an American male bachelor V.P. of sales. He nailed me with,

"My favorite food to make is macaroni and cheese."

I gasped, "From a box."

"You got it. Love it."

This is why you must never expect or anticipate with people. You improvise,

"How do you get a box of mac and cheese?"

"Are you serious?"

"Yes. Please help me."

"Okay. First you go to the store –"

I got him. With great relief,

"What do I DO next?"

"Then you go to the macaroni and cheese aisle."

Mission accomplished. Thoughts and phrases. This goes for everybody… accent or no accent. Even for those who love mac and cheese. If you really commit to helping me, you would never leave me behind in the dust.

Being the very best speaker you can be is a partnership with others. Don't run your mouth. Help them. That is what you focus on doing and then everything will change for you. You can begin to do this right now and make it work for you.

Changing speech to remove an accent takes at least two years of dedicated work. I have yet to meet a client daily for two years. We need to change something that will have significant effect in the real world now. Fancy ideas and theories do not work. What I give you is just a reminder of what is real with people.

For those who will commit the time needed, here is a way of changing your speaking on your own. Find a person who has made recordings (audio) who is your idea of how you wish you could speak. A person whom you admire the way they speak. Get an audio recording of them and listen to it over and over and over again. Then mimic their speaking. Verbally impersonate them.

You will find that you have what they are saying memorized and when you feel you are making a good impersonation of their speaking, record yourself doing them. Once you get the vowel and consonant changes down, work on the lilt or music of their speaking. After this is accomplished, speak that way in casual situations with friends or family. You will eventually be able to change the way you speak and talk like the person you admire. I had to do this on the spot and under the gun in my true tale titled 15 Hours From Midnight.

For those who like to micromanage, do not break your speech up into a bunch of phrases and thoughts. It will become unnatural and in pieces. Speaking in thoughts and phrases is in your action and intention of helping. Do not try to mechanically break things down. Trust that you are committed to what you are doing and then just let it move, flow, and change. The change is not in making a breakdown. The change is in you.

If you can get me to understand how to make your favorite dish, or how to drive to your home, you can do this right now. I have spent many years in the simplicity of getting people to understand what they already know.

Remember. The correct effective pace at which you speak is not determined by the speaker. It is determined by who is listening to you.

Kids and teens are in an epidemic of speaking so fast, their mouth is being trained by texting.

If we tell our teenagers to not talk so fast, maybe we should walk the talk.

Breathing Is Healthy

I miss a dear friend and mentor, David Hooks, whom I had the privilege of meeting in NYC, when I was starting to break into professional theatre and he was attempting to break out. David founded major repertory and regional theatres while performing in over four hundred productions. That must be a record. It is no longer possible to do that many plays. At the time, after his service in the Navy during WWII, he began non-stop acting in the thriving days of a season of repertory theatre followed by the old summer stock play every two weeks.

David was an intellectual book worm, from all of the days of low pay "on the road" hotel rooms. He had done every major Shakespearean role, usually more than once. He had read all classic literature and to my amazement he could actually remember what he read.

I got an "F" in bonehead biology class. I deserved it. Every time I laid down to read that huge heavy textbook, when I reached page three and the word "protoplasm", that big book would hit me in the face. Every time. No better sleeping pill was ever developed than that biology textbook. I now look upon the field of protoplasm as a fine resting place.

For some quaint reason, David liked to talk with me. I would say something clever and he would tell me the complicated name of some foreign guy who said the same thing centuries ago. He found great amusement in this.

So one fine intellectual afternoon, between his chain smoking and guzzling coffee, David drew an actor's expressive breath and addressed me in clipped "standard English" for the stage,

"Dennis."

My cue to sit poised for his next line. His elocution projected,

"How in the world do you teach acting?"

I waited for the next line developing the conflict. He fed me,

"I dare say that I would not have the foggiest idea of where to begin."

That wrong line threw me good. I spoke under pressure,

"Whaaat!"

He gave me the stage. I chortled on,

"This coming from one who has done 400 plays!" Ready to thrust my rapier, "You dare to put that to me!"

Satisfied that we were now drawn into comedic relief, David resolved,

"I have always hired actors who already knew what to do."

I now had my opening for the exposition, and theme of this plot,

"Alas good sir. If... you were to teach acting...what would be the first and most important subject to begin working on?"

"Breathing," said without a moment of hesitation and in full conviction.

This from a lifetime in the theatre. The first and foremost thing to achieve success in any performance is something we do non-stop twenty-four hours a day, or do we?

What kind of nonsense is this? Most certainly, this writer and that old actor have broken their legs one too many times. Why, if we no longer breathe, we die! Period!

I get that. I am not talking about "ceasing breathing." I am talking about "not breathing." All People do that out of habit every day of their lives at times. Some even turn this habit into a form of emotional expression. At times of:

"You're next!" Followed by a "gasp" of sucking in air that holds back the breathing. Or,

"In my office—now!" or

"Who did this?" or

"Relax!" etc.

Does emotion change our breathing pattern? As when catching our breath when crying; or becoming breathless when laughing uncontrollably; or when huffing and puffing when in a rage.

At these times, is our breathing controllable? No. That is what makes these moments natural. That is what makes these moments so special and true. When we are at our most moving with other people. At these moments of passion, emotion is clear and free. Our heart overpowers our head. Try to stop laughing when laughing uncontrollably and you will begin to choke and laugh hysterically. Logic goes out the window. The attention of others is drawn to us like a magnet.

When in a rage, the air huffing and puffing out will ignite and flames will shoot out of our nostrils and ears.

If breathing is such a powerful result of emotional reaction, why can't breathing become a powerful influence on emotional reaction?

It absolutely can be. We just are not used to deliberately using it in that manner. It is natural but not normal that way. Have you ever said to someone appearing tense,

"Breathe. Take it easy. Take a breath."

This is a natural process. We just forget about it. Most of us used to be babies. Can a baby appear relaxed? Is it possible for a baby's face to appear authentic? Do we question if a baby has pretense?

We all have this ability; we just lost it along the way. It is too obvious, so let's recover it. How important is breathing?

First let's check to see if you have developed incorrect breathing habits. In comfortable privacy, stand and inhale breathing. (Not a huge dramatic breath—just normal). As you inhale, look to see what part of you is moving. It will be one of three areas your shoulders, your chest, or your tummy near your belt buckle area. If your shoulders rose and moved while inhaling, you are breathing incorrectly. Your voice will be higher and tenser than it should be. You will also have a tendency to quickly get hoarse, scratchy throat, or even lose your voice. That is because your voice is being supported by tension in your throat and shoulders, mechanically squeezing the speaking out of you.

If your chest moves while inhaling, your breathing is incorrect. Your voice will have a tendency to become "breathy" and higher in pitch. You will lack resonance in your voice. It will be difficult to speak longer passages.

If your breath is doing one of the above, you actually do not know what your true voice sounds like and can be. When people first hear their own voice from video playback, they wonder if the microphone is broken.

Some years ago, I coached an eleven year-old boy in camera acting. Upon seeing and hearing himself for the first time, the boy fell off of his chair laughing. After his fit of laughter, I asked,

"What is so funny?"

Well, "I always thought (made his voice low) I spoke like my dad."

His smile exploded, "But instead (made his voice high in falsetto) I sound like a girl!"

Unless you have watched and listened to your playbacks, you do not know how you sound to others.

If your belt-buckle tummy area was the only part that moved when you inhaled and exhaled, you are breathing correctly. Do not say this is new to you. You breathed exactly this way when you were a baby. This is the breathing "technique" you already came issued with. You do not need to study this.

Can a baby cry for a long time without losing their voice or asking for throat drops? Does a baby's natural breathing make them look tense and not ready to speak?

How did we get so messed up? It wasn't the pureed bananas. It was more like the phone receiver, as if smooshing the other person's ear against our mouth.

David's Father was an old-fashioned country doctor in the hills of North Carolina. He delivered most of the babies at their own homes, arriving in a horse and buggy. Frankly, I deeply wish that I would have lived in the simplicity of that not so long ago time. So let's go back to those days of no smart phone in every back pocket.

Let your name be Hatfield and my name will be McCoy. We have settled our differences and put away our long guns. The running creek that separates our properties flows between the two of our homes. I have important news to tell you, as we stand on each side of the sounds of the babbling brook between us.

How am I going to speak to you over the rushing creek? First, I will take in a breath. It will come from my belly because I already know the other ways of breathing won't "be a reachin' you." When I do speak, I better say each and every word deliberately without rushing or you won't understand me. As I speak to you, I will "receive" (let in) whether or not you get my thoughts and meanings. Since this is a book about speaking, you just got your belly full of how to do it.

Don't get complicated with fancy theories about speaking. The Hatfield and McCoys here did not need a speaking coach —they needed a shooting coach.

Try speaking across the creek like a machine gun mouth teen and see what happens. You will probably start a war from frustration.

Go back to where you began this life—breathe.

Before you begin your speaking, presentation, meeting, or any activity with pressure—anything—do this first—breathe into relaxing—relax into breathing. That is your beginning action. What you do before you begin anything. This is totally natural.

Focus is doing only one thing at a time—fully. Focus only on your breathing if you feel nervous or anxious. This will help take your mind away from the harmful and unnecessary distractions. Always do this as your very first action.

Before you enter or go in, focus on regulating your breathing. It is futile to try to work on anything at this point of time. You are out of time to prepare. Just prior to entrance, your physical condition is more important than anything else. If you really feel anxious or nervous, you really need to mechanically regulate your breathing pattern back to normal (or it's impossible to appear normal).

Everyone who you are about to meet also has a history of breathing. If you enter breathing, you will appear natural, normal, relaxed and at ease. If you enter "not breathing", you will appear tense in the face and in movement. Your not breathing will cause you to appear not natural and not normal (because you are not). I am not being cute and thinking this up. It is just "being human part one." A kid could spot this and remark, "They look weird."

No fancy breathing practices are required. Just inhale gently from your belt buckle tummy area and gently exhale through your nose and mouth. You do not have to study this. But if you have severe habitual behavior built up to the contrary, you will need to consciously do this for a while to replace the harmful habit.

If you go out in the morning to start your car, how about warming up the cold engine for just a bit, whether it needs it or not. We don't have to fire it up and slam it into gear and stomp on the pedal. Ease in and ease out. Warm it up and treat yourself with at least as much care as you would your car.

It is easy to fall into the trap of looking at the artificiality of speaking under different formats and unconsciously tossing out the simple human actions that come natural to our functioning. The format may be artificial but you must be natural.

My old friend David, who started as Hamlet and then finished as King Lear, placed breathing above all else. This is important because we are all human.

This chapter is to define the term breathing. We will refer to this in many other lessons such as "cold reading" and "getting your emotion on cue" and "making an entrance." No matter how busy you are, you have plenty of time to practice regulating your breathing.

No matter your schedule—you have twenty-four hours every day. To breathe.

Movement on Stage or Before Others Looking at You

This chapter only covers physical movement, by one speaker on a stage or in an area in front of others, either live or recorded by video device. If speaking only from behind a podium, please review the section on "cold reading".

First, the areas of the stage, when "center stage", facing your audience—

The area to your left is known as "stage left."

The area approaching the audience is called "downstage."

The area behind you, away from the audience is known as upstage."

I include this in case you should receive or communicate stage direction at some time. You do not need to be on a stage. You just need to be in front of people.

Audience directions are opposite from their point of view, so this can be confusing. Instead, let's just use these acceptable terms, from your point of view facing your audience—

"look center" "look left" "look right"

Looking out over all areas of your audience will be known as "covering your audience." When you do this, you are pointing your eyes at each area. It is not staring. Touching each area with your eyes will establish connection with your audience.

When moving on stage, it is called "cross right (or left)" and "move up (or down). This will keep you from wasting your time in confusion when given stage direction by a professional. By the way, if some video director should shoot terms at you like "camera left" etc, that is a sign they are either inexperienced or just out of film school and showing off. Those directions are for the crew and will only confuse you performing. Demand they speak in your terms, which would tell you to "move to your left" etc.

The chief enemies of effective movement on stage are—

Too much movement

Moving too fast

Moving for no reason

Wandering the stage while speaking

Fidgeting movement

Allowing your energy and excitement to push or propel you

Steps that are too big

Stop-go-stop-go etc.

Here is a basic solution for all of the above and more. You will get the hang of it and then adapt and adjust to your own needs and conditions.

1. Grab yourself a piece of paper and a pencil. Draw a rectangle or whatever is the shape of your stage or area where you stand to face others.

2. Make dots where it would be best for you to be standing area center and to your right and left, which should be roughly middle depth.

3. Make another dot a few steps towards your audience from your center mark.

4. Then make another dot upstage center, where you would be in good position to support any visuals behind and above you.

5. If you connect the dots, you will have two uneven triangles, back to back.

6. The dots are not exact spots marking where to stand. They only help define a small area of movement.

7. Now, keep your movement on stage from any dot area to any other dot area.

Please note. Think of this as simplifying and subtracting other stage areas. Do not think of this as stiff rules of where to stand on stage. We are narrowing down the stage to the best areas for you during your message. Once you get the hang of this—free it up.

Whenever you reach a dot area with crossing or movement

Stop.

Settle.

Grab everyone's attention in this new position

The stop itself will draw attention and give itself importance.

Feet apart comfortably (check this ladies-do not keep your legs and feet together.

Flat feet. fifty-fifty weight on both feet. Solid platform.

If you are going to move—move.

If you are going to stop—stop.

Don't move while you are stopping.

Covering your audience

If standing stage right—look more to your left than right.

If standing stage left—look more to your right than left.

If center—make sure you look all three directions or some will feel excluded

Use the area down center when you want to hit the audience with a special point, by coming closer to them a few steps. This will add emphasis.

Use the upstage area only for supporting your visuals behind you. Never say anything "super special" upstage. If you want to emphasize, move a few steps down, closer to the audience.

When you cross from area to area, do not let your energy and excitement "sweep" you at high speed. Instead, move slowly and evenly when crossing. It will feel kind of like a "country stroll."

If you have a tendency to move fast or quickly, try moving "at half speed" even if it does not feel normal (is being on stage normal?). If they are recording you and you are in a waist up camera shot, a fast cross on stage will look like you are sailing through the air. A static camera angle, panning sideways, accelerates the apparent speed of movement on screen.

Move slow—even—smooth

With hand gestures—smaller—rounder—smoother.

For those who like to micro-manage, do not choreograph yourself a ballet.

Once you get a bit used to this and do it without thought, you may even use movement on stage to deliberately enhance what you are speaking about. Such as:

Pause.

Take two very short steps down stage, as you connect while covering your audience.

Then stop—settle—grab their attention.

Entrance Tips for an Interview, Audition, or Meeting Face to Face

Here are simple tips and reminders in a procedure list for entrance.

Before you knock on the door, regulate your breathing. That is your only focus. There is nothing better or more important to do at this point.

Make sure you inhale when going through the door. Your face will then appear relaxed and at ease and normal. This is the first visual impression of you. This is the first impression meeting before the meeting.

Allow yourself to feel "friendly" to begin a relationship.

Connect visually with whoever is in the room you have just entered. Make sure that your eyes have touched everyone else's eyes.

Do not charge into the room. Stroll in. Walk in a straight line towards your place. If you are holding your breath, you will move too fast.

Do your best not to talk while you walk in (some situations may cause exception to this, such as if they actively engage you).

Instead, stop-settle-grab their attention. If they are not looking at you, such as looking down at some notes, do not speak until they look at you. It does no good to talk to the top of a person's head. They will look up, if for no other reason than to see why you are not talking.

Do not jabber. Three distinct separated important statements of introduction, something like –

"My name is _____" then separate -

"and" (use to separate clearly and emphasize your introduction)

"I am here _____ " (simple reason which they already know)

These words, spoken clearly with purpose, have all the needed information and nothing in excess. This will make you sound confident.

I advise you not to say "Hi!" or "Good morning" etc. It is not needed and one more thing that can and often does go wrong.

After you "meet n' greet" them, followed by your first verbal introduction, help them to make a decision on what to do with you, even if it means not using you right now.

After you introduce yourself, prove that you can listen fully. You must prove that you can listen and pay attention. Do not interrupt. Do not think of what to say when they are speaking to you. That is a sign that you do not listen well.

Let them invite you to sit down. After they invite you to sit down, there is only one thing to say, "thank you" (not mechanically said).

Do not ever sit back on the chair. Do not sit rigid in the chair. Just settle in the chair and lead with you eyes a couple of inches towards them.

A common mistake is to lead with your mouth. The indication for this is the chin is up and you are looking down your nose. If someone has this habit (and there are many), it indicates their own self-importance in what they say and appears that way. Always lead with your eyes. That is the human way of leading with the heart.

As you saw in some of my tales in this book, a critical thing to do as soon as possible is "break the ice" with the other person, so the wall of separation is brought down between you. This will not come from a clever joke or a manipulative technique. It will come from a genuine exchange of feelings (small but genuine human feelings). Look for an opening to disarm your own self.

Also, in these times, do not force a handshake. It is like forcing a hug on someone. If they offer, then do not hesitate to respond back. Let them initiate the impulse of what to do.

When the meeting is over, you are no longer in the same relationship as you began with. Adjust to what has changed and then leave them with a "tag" (last feeling you leave them off with). This is a last impression personal signature of your personality that can cause you to be remembered with a feeling.

Reminder. There is no such thing as an ending—there is only the beginning of what happens next. Always use this key perspective in all that you do. Do not quit the meeting in your mind when you think that it is coming to a conclusion.

If your intention is truly to help, others will feel it and you will stand out by this one action, in and of itself.

Every time you are remembered, you have succeeded in making the meeting worthwhile. You have achieved true value of your time together.

Body Language

I have run into two major ways the term "body language" is being used. One of which has grown into a myth and the other has always been a great truth pertaining to people.

First the myth = looking at a human and analyzing from their body positions for what is going on inside them with consistent accuracy. This is hooptedoodle.

If a human's reactions are completely spontaneous or if their behavior is totally candid, this first form of "reading" a person could be valid to a point. However, these two big "ifs" fall under the category of the second type of "body language," which I will cover later this chapter.

During the past week of writing this chapter, I have had two clients break out in a disturbed expression physically appearing as suffering. This happened in our private session, which was going well. So what did that graphic "body language" mean? It meant in both cases that their allergies were acting up severely from the change of weather. So much for pin-point analysis of their body language.

This "technique of body language" is used in live theatre, such as in a production outside in a park, where some of the audience is fifty yards away from the stage performance. The play has to be projected out at a distance. The actor's body positions are used to help project the actions and feelings of the characters because we cannot see very well at that distance.

But if we can see you, up close and personal, such as face-to-face or on-camera, then your using your body to convey feelings and actions will be like the acting used in old silent movies. We now consider this overacting and posing. This type of acting, which was referred to as "representational or presentational acting style" is out dated by our naturalistic taste in modern believability.

Just as a skilled villain can beat a "lie detector test," so can someone use the "technique of body language" to deceive an observer using "the technique of over-rated analysis."

I have a friend who is a U.S. Marshal. He told me about a top expert from "Justice" who is charged with determining truth or a lie in major cases. This top expert in law enforcement interrogations admitted to –

"On our very best day, we can maybe tell if someone is really lying—50% of the time."

I would believe this expertise and real-life experience, rather than someone who dreams up fancy theory on how to analyze accurately all humans using their perception of "body language."

People do arbitrary things, at times, for no reason whatsoever.

"Why did you do that?"

"I have no idea. I just did it."

Let's get to the good stuff. What is the truth about our body? Here is the principle, not the rule, the principle in my simple way defines –

"The inside moves the outside."

This was the foundation of body language, before it got complicated into voodoo. As you can read from my writings, I do not believe in "perfection" when it comes to people. This principle works, as close to perfectly with people, as anything else ever will. A principal is an eternal truth.

When a feeling or state of being is not interfered with and the body is given natural freedom to move, you have a stronger impact than just speaking. There used to be a television show based on this called "Candid Camera." The candid reactions and silent behavior of people needs no subtitles to understand.

If you were to go off in a rage with fire pouring out of your nostrils, would anyone come up to you and say,

"Wow! You were really mad. But next time hold up your left arm at this angle instead and we will get clearer meaning from your body language."

Movement does not necessarily mean movement. I once saw an acting teacher watch a section of a stage set fall on someone she loved. Her tremendously expressive body language movement was not one hair on her head moved. She was frozen still. People are unpredictable.

Have you ever had anyone get emotional and walk away from you? How much did their back say? You did not need subtitles.

Based on my own experience, I think the part that gives people away the most is the spontaneous moving feeling from their eyes, or their hands.

If you wish to enhance your expression, you already have the ability. Just use your body with trust and honesty. If you wish to express or enhance your speaking, allow your inside to move your outside freely.

Spontaneity or improvisation is freedom of movement, emotionally and physically, within a form. Without form, you have chaos. Compelling movement before others is an extension of expression, not an extension of energy.

The Pause

Now we come to the famous "pause." The mistake here is the same as with "physical gesture." It is misunderstood as being mechanical and external. I have heard people say they were instructed to "take a two beat pause" or "take a meaningful pause."

The pause comes internally from the speaker or it will not only seem mechanical, but also appear manipulative and worked by technique.

The two basic reasons for the pause are to separate and/or to sink in.

The pause used to separate is for emphasis and usually occurs before the point the speaker wants to make special.

The pause used to sink in is usually after the point is spoken. This is best done when written as a partnership between speaker and their audience. The speaker makes special the point they just made and the audience is given the pause to let it settle in from their own perspective and experience.

Both of these pauses can occur in the middle of a phrase to serve the same functions.

Do not "do a pause" by counting or using mechanical means. This is not an effective pause; it is a time lapse. I find that a manipulative use of the pause is really irritating and insulting to the intelligence of the audience. I have actually seen this done by someone who teaches it.

The pause is done at times when used around a word that emphasizes what is to follow is important to listen to. Such words are –

But "I'll give you the money – but -"

If "I'll give you the money – if –"

Other words used like this are **so** and **etc.**

If you choose to deliberately inject the pause, it is always done internally from feelings to be effective. The pause is active not passive. During the action of the pause, you are in full connection with your listener and you are receiving (letting them in).

The length of the pause is determined by your feel of your listener. They are not watching or hearing you make a meaningful pause. They are actively participating in the pause. You set it up—they make it. The pause is from them—with them—and for them. When you do the pause this way, it has power, with your audience. It is alive and in true relationship with the people listening to you.

Connect with Others

Without contact, there is no connection. Without connection, there is no relationship. Instead of speaking to someone, you will be speaking at them.

Here again we are implementing action that you already do in your life's experience on a daily basis with people. However, much of the time in the real world we leave out these natural actions, taking them for granted.

If you were washing the dishes after dinner, and a family member came into the kitchen asking you a routine question; would you stop washing, turn to squarely face them, and look them square in the eyes as you clearly speak your reply? Most every day relationship is taken for granted. In times of crisis or deep involvement, behavior is different.

If a child (you care about), rushes up to you in a disturbed emotional state, the first thing you do is look at them and receive (let in and sense their feelings). If you are caught off guard (spontaneous), your own vulnerability reacts from your perspective (father, mother, friend, etc.). You may speak to them (not at them) and it will usually be simple,

"Are you okay?" or "What's wrong?"

Then you simply listen and receive, because your action has now become the all-important priority of helping. No one needs to train in this. Unless you are a sociopath, this emotional chip is already planted in your heart.

When I was a young rascal lad serving time at "stinkin' Lincoln" grade school, I would unjustly be sent to the principal's office. She usually did not know what I did. This lady warden, just sat me down and those steel German blue eyes pierced into my soul and my shoes. Not a word was spoken. Just hard drilling contact with drilling third degree connection. I would give in and confess. After which, I got shaken like a paint can in the hardware store, which is likely why I now have so many loose fillings in my teeth.

First you must have contact. You cannot hit your target unless you see it. This is the sign that you are really with others individually or with a group. Unlike routine life, you must do this to give others recognition, purpose, and presence.

This leads to connection. You receive them by letting them in freely and openly. After this, a relationship can be created, even with a stranger, when you allow a feeling or emotional reaction to occur.

Okay so what is the big deal? The big deal is to establish a connection with others before you even open your mouth.

Most do not do this. Because they take it for granted when in front of one or a group or on-camera. Never listen to anyone telling you to "get moving and cut to the chase." Your audience will end up having to chase you. If you do not make contact and connection with others before you begin to speak, they may not walk out on you or throw rotten fruit at you; but you will begin separate and segregated from those you wish to reach.

It only takes seconds to do this. Do not treat it as a chore (wrong perspective). You only need just a touch of desire. When anyone leaves this natural process off, they have a perspective that what they are doing is artificial. All we are doing is the natural action of "meetin' n' greetin' folks. Leave it off and you remain a stranger.

I am a firm believer in the importance of beginnings. The beginning colors what follows and points the direction of a new relationship. The tone and mode of what follows is needed for the best speaking. Are you putting so much emphasis on the content that you overlook the impact of the beginning and end? First impression and last impression are critical, especially with people you have not met before.

All you need to do is just do this natural process when beginning. You don't need to study this, you simply need to not forget it. Do not take who you are speaking to for granted. You will then draw others to you upon first contact and begin a true connection with each other. Then lead them where you want.

Now you can begin your relationship with them.

Relationship with Others

Relationship. Some cringe at the sound of the dreaded "R-Word."

Since we are defining our terms, let's contain relationship to reflect only the results of one of the most basic and advanced principles of acting on-camera or on stage. Here is how you create relationship in front of others.

"When you look at—or towards—a person, place, or thing —with a feeling—it reads relationship to your audience."

We have been trained in this principle from our first television, movies, or plays that we have watched. The feeling of the actor/character reflects the emotional quality of the relationship we see. Do not confuse this with real life, where I might be angry and frustrated and be facing towards some arbitrary direction, for no reason whatsoever. I just happened to be facing in that direction.

But if I am in front of people or an audience; they have been trained that everything has meaning. If I am in a television drama and glance down at a gun (fake prop in reality) while I am feeling sad and depressed, the viewers will gasp "uh-oh! He's thinking about shooting himself." If I am in front of an audience and look at the actor playing my grandmother with a feeling of happy and warm, everyone watching will say something like, "he loves his grandma."

It is how an audience responds to what goes on in front of them, whether on stage, on-screen, or during anything presented.

So relationship is how you give value and emotional quality to your connection.

What if I am introduced by someone whom I despise? No better tool than this. If you feel happy and friendly and aim the feeling in their general direction, not even looking directly at them, the audience will read that you have a good friendly relationship. If you don't believe this, put this book down and go watch some television. You will see it throughout any show. Even in a crummy show, you will see the proof of this audience/ viewer principle.

I'm going in front of a group of strangers, who not only do not know me, they don't even care about me. There isn't any relationship between us.

Okay. How about tonight at midnight going to a bad section of town. Find a dark alley. Go into the dark alley until you run into a stranger. You are now very much in a specific relationship.

You may say, "My content is serious—not emotional with feelings."

First, there is a difference between "serious" and "somber." Next, if you are presenting yourself to humans, a lack of feelings may cause you to be known as having the personality of a rock.

Do not confuse emotional feeling with extremes such as crying or foaming at the mouth. Like most things, the answer may be in the middle. Your feelings need to move, flow, change; even with subtlety.

I like saying dumb things to my classes. They always remember the dumb things I say and usually quote them more accurately. How is this for poetic imagery?

"If it moves—it's alive…if it doesn't move—it's dead."

That's a dumb phrase; but is this the truth?

If you have feelings and are forcing them (to act like you are happy), and they do not move, flow, or change, in a natural manner, it will read to the audience as either "a mood" or "phony." The dumbest human in the audience has a PhD in feelings granted from their own life's experiences.

In another chapter, I will show you how to get more emotional, on cue.

Whenever you enter before others, as you face them, the feeling that you express will be read as your relationship with them. It is that simple. When you face a person or a group and you feel happy and friendly while looking at or even towards them, you will establish a friendly relationship with them at that moment.

Many times on a stage you cannot even see the audience because of the blinding stage lighting. That does not matter. You simply aim your eyes towards the audience areas of left-center-right and you will read having a relationship with all of them. Your audience will feel contact, connection, and relationship, before you open your mouth to speak.

Look at some movies or television, you will see some close up shots featuring an actor's reactions. If that actor is competent, they will clearly appear to be with the other actor in the scene, even though we may not see the other character in the shot. If they stink as an actor, they will look like a solo head from lack of connection.

Determine what relationship you wish to have the audience perceive and then make a commitment to begin to feel that way. Then look at or towards the person, place or thing, and aim the feeling in that direction. Your audience will believe that feeling as what is going on between the two. This is a principle for on-camera acting.

When I produced and/or directed over forty-six plays, we would have an invited free pre-opening performance for my acting classes. We would gain valuable feedback from them as a test audience. After the play, what was of most importance to the audience was:

Relationship • Relationship • Relationship

That is simple to understand. The lights are fake, the sets are fake, everything is fake except one thing—the feelings of the humans in the show. A human hears the dialogue, but follows the feelings. That is needed to believe and become involved. In order to believe the feelings you need to trust. Whether you borrow money from someone or listen to their presentation, how important is trust? Who trusts phony or empty relationships? Who trusts technique driven speaking?

Trust comes from relationship. I can respect who you are and I can be interested in what you have…but…if I don't trust you and maybe not even like you; how can we even begin?

CHANGING YOUR FOCUS
Some Butterscotch Detectives

There are many flavors of ice cream. Some are labeled with complicated exotic flavors reflecting our times. But vanilla, chocolate, and strawberry, still survive the turning calendars. These classics still remain at the top of the lists.

There are fewer flavors of private detectives, who are more concerned with surviving the rent today, rather than surviving a dark alley. Staples of P.I. work has been hardboiled down to the likes of insurance fraud with neck braces, leg work for attorneys, and divorce surveillance. The romance of adventure is becoming rare.

I would have none of that routine work and chose to side with the few remaining butterscotch private detectives. Butterscotch is an old fashioned flavor, still around, but harder to find. This breed was what I called "the knock on the door detectives." A now dying breed, who still conducted trouble as their business. They are a walking hangover, who still answered the soft or frantic knock on the door, leading them to trouble. I look back on a few with great warmth and nostalgia.

There was my buddy "old Aff," an old timer whom I deeply enjoyed chatting with over a jar of scotch. He began in WWII as an O.S.S. Agent (Office of Strategic Services which was the forerunner to the C.I.A.). Once we went for some shooting practice and I uncovered why he always wore cowboy boots under his suit. His left cowboy boot doubled as a concealed holster for a well-worn Colt 1903, 32 caliber automatic. This small flat pistol was the kind often whipped out in the old black and white film noir movies.

Old Aff, should have stuck with answering the door to trouble. One time he got so excited over the pay to photograph an accident scene, he bought a new little camera. Unfortunately, his pistol was loaded but the camera was not. So much for getting too excited over the pictures and the pay.

Then there was Roger the retired F.B.I. agent. Once he was hired for a missing person and called on a favor from some (shall we say) former colleagues. He located the person in San Francisco. The problem was, with the aid of his so-called friends, it only took fifteen minutes to find the guy. There was a business concern of great service not equaling the compensation value. So I think Roger went boating for a bit before timely notifying the client.

As Roger was a part of the JFK assassination investigation, I attempted to schmooze him to give me the inside confidential "primary poop." Though I provided the scotch (not of the butter type), in true government fashion, all I got was a recording.

Just one more for the road was Toro, who was a former Mexican Federale. Being too good and too honest gave him the reward of a bomb explosion of his home in Mexico City. Toro wisely and quickly moved he and his family for a hiatus in Southern California, minus the dynamite.

Their family home was now a 1920's built house in East Los Angeles. Entering through the front door placed you in a cozy small living room typical of the houses of that period. To the right was the small dining alcove. But instead of a dining table, sat an old large wooden desk. Dead center facing the desk was a wood straight back chair for clients, like used in the old library days. I later found out why this guest chair was centered facing the old desk.

On the other side of the desk, just above Toro's chair, was a hand made concealed shelf. Taking a snooze on this shelf was a custom Pachmayr 45 Automatic pistol with the business end of the gun pointed dead center at the guest seat.

I wonder how many of you would like this type of ergonomic office furniture? After all, if your door is open, who knows who will end up across the business desk from you. Maybe they don't like butterscotch.

Licensed private investigators are not a favorite flavor of the police and slightly less popular with the doers of wrong. Unlike the police force, there are no rookie P.I.s. You have to have a lot of experience before you can even qualify to take the California Bureau of Investigative Services state test for licensing.

The area separating the blue police line and the off-color criminal line can certainly take a shade of gray. Police unions work their best to disarm the P.I.s. Not because of the danger of gunfire, rather, because of the profit of off-duty police guns and police officers moonlighting for extra money. With an off-duty gun comes a badge. Thus, there is a bit more security in the hired security.

Some police moonlighting may take the form of "bounty hunting."

After being arrested, some misunderstood soul may have reasonable bail set in arraignment at the local court. The accused may post the amount of bail and then walk out the front door instead of the rear door, which leads back to a jail cell. This posted bail bond is to assure those concerned that the accused will obey the court order to return for their trial. Sometimes, the misunderstood soul misunderstands this and confuses temporary release with a "get out of jail free card." In this game of life, this freed soul then "skips" out on bail posted by now former friends and family or a bail bond company, to pursue getting lost in the shuffle.

The bounty hunter finds and retrieves the now mistrusted soul and returns them to their rightful jail cell. For much of this hunting expedition requested by a worried bail bond company, who are less interested in the dramatics and potential tragedies of hiring a private bounty hunter/P.I. there is a safer solution; just get some friendly police to quietly pick up the fugitive. Now everyone has a happy ending except the offender, including any police who may also profit a bit.

With the unpredictability of life on the street, the chips may not fall and the cookie may not crumble this way. That is when the private bounty hunter joins the chase for those "pulling a runner."

In the "city of la la," I had the privilege of getting to know and sharing more than a few cocktails with the most notorious bounty hunter of our time. His nom de plume for our "fanciful" purposes will be "Mr. Hunter."

Mr. Hunter sported the beard of the fifty-dollar bill dead president and must have weighed over two hundred fifty pounds. He was not quite as wide as he was tall. This made him rather deadly in a scuffle. All he would have to do is charge you like a freight train in shoes. You would then be smashed into the wall, leaving an indelible business footprint in the sheetrock. Even a black belt would not get in a good kick before becoming as flat as a crumpled fifty-dollar bill.

All that being said, Mr. Hunter, always struck me as being a warm, genuine, likeable man; and I would trust him playing Santa. The making of peace with someone he had just handcuffed, is quite a lesson in business public relations and diplomacy. He once told me that many a time out of state police would deliberately throw him into the same jail cell with his captured fugitive. Different states have a different sense of humor. Certainly this is a shining example of how an uncomfortable business fit requires immediate connection and respectful relationship established, followed by a compelling presentation of strategic content.

However, there are times when even charm will not quell the winter of our discontent. Mr. Hunter had a medical history of being shot and stabbed numerous times (I seem to recall the number 8 for some reason but maybe I have that confused with a Chinese fortune cookie lucky number). He also told me his ribs, both short and adamic, were broken or cracked, at various times other than holidays. Mr. Hunter was big and tough, and knew the score, so I remember him as confident and at peace. It's the little guys or short men who can turn real mean on you. Maybe they have fewer ribs issued.

Mr. Hunter always carried concealed a Smith&Wesson airweight Chief's Special 38 revolver. This is the smallest of the more serious gats. For decades, police detectives carried these "snub nosed" 38s. Because of his wide girth, Mr. Hunter had a natural made holster for this little gun at the top of the mounds of his behind (teen girls call this "butt crack" for some reason having to do with constantly pulling up their pants). Thus, nestled in this natural crevasse, the hide out gun was kept warm and safe from falling out in public. If I attempted this, being without the necessary and proper endowment, the 38 would slide down and end up in my sock.

He once confided in me, "If I thought there might be real trouble, I'd carry my Colt 45 Gold Cup Automatic." I also owned the same in a National Match model and it never did jam on me.

One evening, over melting ice, Mr. Hunter reminisced,

"One time I was talking with this guy, over a table—a cocktail table like this one." His eyes melted to the wistful whim of regret as he continued, "The guy got real quiet" (what did I tell you about watching out for when men get real quiet) "Then, he stood up slowly as he reached."

Some memories past bring up that melancholy,

"He pulled a knife. I pulled this little 38. I emptied the gun dead center chest. Five shots in the X ring."

He sighed with a sadness,

"He still stuck me with the blade. Got me good. I learned my lesson."

That was my cue to ask, "What was that?"

"Next time. Shoot him in the head."

The wisdom passed on in this book comes from expensive experience.

Always pay attention to your opponent's hands, rather than what they say. It is hard for them to pull a knife with their mouth. There will be a demonstration of this in the chapter, "Showdown At Venus."

LESSON LEARNED

In serious business or social encounters, up close and personal, stopping your opponent immediately is more important than laying them to rest. Winning loses a lot of fun, when you still get stuck in the belly.

The Deadly Busboy

Toro, the former Mexican Federale, slowly removed his custom 45 automatic pistol from behind his desk; it was professional courtesy not to leave it aimed at me, while I sat in the chair in front of his old wooden desk. It is nice to be trusted.

This Mexican P.I. had too many open case files. I had volunteered to help lighten his workload. With his best "amigo smile," he held up a hand full of files,

"Any particular kind?"

I stayed with butterscotch, "Any flavor you chose."

As in poker, Toro dealt a file off the top of the deck. He spoke like a dentist,

"This is a good one for you. We just…"

The word "just" can make my ears wiggle,

"We just want to confirm this guy is working at this high class restaurant."

He passed me the file with the address and a crummy snapshot of the young Mexican man. I wondered,

"He looks too young to be a chef."

"No. A busboy."

"I'm listening…shoot."

Toro paused and sat back in his office chair (another sign to pay very close attention). He carefully chose his words (still another sign),

"He left Mexico in a hurry. He murdered some guy."

"Poison salsa?"

Toro smiled, "This is what I like so much about you Dennis. You have a great sense of fun."

"Yeah. I'm just a walking fiesta."

The next day, I held the 357 Combat Magnum revolver and pushed the cylinder release latch. The round revolver cylinder flipped out and I proceeded to load "six beans in the wheel."

It was still a hot brown day in Los Angeles (L.A.). Heading west to Beverly Hills (B.H.), along Santa Monica Boulevard, I was occupied by memorizing the picture and description of our deadly busboy.

I planned on spotting the fugitive after 2:30pm. When I was a teen, I worked as a busboy and that is when lunch shift is usually over.

I parked my car on the street (no expense money for valet). As I would be walking into and around a lunch crowd of people, I chose to leave my gun in the trunk of my car. At the time, that type of revolver looked like an American police gun. I did not want a 45 auto, as the busboy would know that in Mexico only Federales can carry a 45. I didn't want to confuse him into thinking that I was some sort of Federale from L.A.'s Little Tokyo. So I left the heat in the car, as I was covertly only "making him" and the most he might be armed with would be stolen silverware.

Nearing this chez Beverly Hills eats, I turned the blind corner of a bush lined sidewalk. One guess who I bumped into? We almost collided. I backed up from the familiar Mexican young man wearing black levis and a sort of ironed white shirt with a black bow tie hanging from the unbuttoned open collar. Criminals and police tend to be suspicious and are not big on coincidences. Crime is a serious business. As in any serious business meeting, it is always best to look not at, but into another person's eyes. The busboy studied the far inside of my eyeballs.

From my end of this chance encounter, I could feel that he was no ordinary member of the hotel and restaurant worker's union. He stood very still and real quiet. His empty hands did not move. It was my move—at spitting distance.

I regretted not having listened to my parents and learned how to speak Japanese. But I bet his parents never gave him Japanese lessons in Mexico City. Since freezing can get you killed, I took immediate action. I bowed to him and apologized in Tokyo city stereotype,

"So sorry."

I was hoping that some old racist movies had made it to Mexico. After another bow to the Mexican busboy, I bestowed another one on him,

"So sorry."

A disgusted feeling twisted the busboy's face. This is called "breaking the ice in social encounters." He pushed ahead, mumbling something about,

"Cabron."

As he stomped away, I know better than to look behind to check him out. He would be looking behind again to check me. Besides, I needed to look no further.

LESSON LEARNED

The next time you go out to eat—who will be serving you water? Careful.

Which brings us "Private Eyes to Venus"

Showdown at Venus

Old lessons say, "Never walk into a place called Mom's" and "Never drink in a place called Venus." I somehow forgot one of those lessons.

The first definition of Venus is the Roman myth, Goddess of Love and Beauty."

The second definition of Venus, as a plant deadly to humans, filled with carbon dioxide, is a more fitting definition of a club called Venus in the north of Hollywood. Why the Association of Licensed Private Investigators group would choose this joint as a fine place for a Christmas party, is beyond my ken.

When I was bartending to help pay the rent, I learned that bartenders hated to work Christmas office parties. There would always be violence. Usually two men and one woman would be responsible for the festivities. I was taught never go "over the bar" to break up a fight. If you do, never turn your back on the femme fatale, or you will soon be rewarded with a high heel shoe spiked on the top of your head.

Back to club Venus. It was a rather unruly celebration from the beginning. I was sitting quietly after having somehow insulted the belly dancer. On one side of me sat Mr. Bounty Hunter and on the other side sat two big scary looking twins with shaved heads and dangerous eyes. They kind of looked like toxic versions of Mr. Clean. One of the two was a famous wrestler in the early 60's, who always wore a mask to scare the audience. Now, some twenty years later, he no longer needed a mask to scare others. It was rumored that the two twins preferred their suspects to resist them to add to the fun of taking them into custody. They liked to rumble.

This club had a small stage above our tables. A young man dressed in a circus type cowboy outfit stood on stage twirling cowboy six shooter guns, one in each hand. He showed off his quick draw in front of the motley crowd. He announced an encore. A challenge was thrown out to our group for anyone to come up and draw against him in a showdown. A Hollywood cowboy style showdown.

There was a brief moment of silence from this collection of cautious Private Eyes until the masked wrestler growled,

"What about Sakamoto! He'll get in the ring with you!"

That opened up the ball. A few tables away sat a middle-aged investigator who still had some acne. He always cherished resentment of me because I always spoke nicely to his two slinky female operatives, causing them to smile. His jealousy loudly egged on,

"Yeah! An Oriental cowboy!" Ha Ha.

Laughter now became contagious throughout our lubricated group. Mr. Hunter did not laugh out loud. You see, this Hollywood gunslinger, who continued to twirl his six shooters, was "one of his boys." Having been shot and stabbed so many times as a bounty hunter had instilled a certain change in his modus operandi. He now exercised business delegation. There were no shortage of young studs who wanted association with the fame of working with Mr. Hunter. So now, Mr. Hunter sent these young studs in through the door first to step on the mines. Increasing one's number of birthdays sometimes brings about increasing wisdom.

The loud mouth crowd screamed for my blood. Taunts, laughter, and applause, carried me up to the Venus club stage. I could see in cowboy Bob's eyes the absolute pleasure of lighting me up in front of everybody. I walked up to his lousy grin; the baby gunslinger removed the six-shooter from his right cowboy holster; he held the gun out towards me, butt first. I was sure what he would do next. So sure, that I did not reach for the gun but instead held my palm up as if receiving car keys. Right on cue, he spun the gun around (called the road agent's spin) and then cocked the hammer and shot me right between the eyes, with the click of his empty gun. This was supposed to make a fool of me.

Strategy is how you fight a war. Tactics are how you fight face-to-face. I read enough of his arrogance to see he was cocky and had his mind distracted on the crowd. He was too fast to beat on a straight draw, so I needed to break his focus. I needed to improvise using his own game of ego and showing off.

As he offered the same gun again, I felt a moment of hesitation deliberately to set him up. He fell for it and nodded that he would kindly allow my sorry self to take the gun. I knew I had him. He could be distracted.

I then did something that he did not expect (expectations throw us off). I turned my back to him completely and checked the cylinder of the gun, as if to make sure it was really unloaded with no cartridges in it. He would read this as my fear and insecurity. I could feel he fell for that also. The group started to quiet when I properly checked the gun for safety. Sensing the shift in his audience, the now very cocky gunslinger made fun of me calling out, "It's not loaded."

That reaction was my signal that he was in the condition I wanted him to be in. Still with my back to him, I slipped the gun into my belt across my belly. This is a very fast cross draw at spitting distance. As I pivoted back to face the gunslinger at a slight angle, my right hand was an inch away from the six-gun's grip and my left hand laid on top of the gun's frame, as if holding it in place.

I connected eye-to-eye with him (absolutely important). He was poised to draw in a slight crouch. The very moment I stopped my angle to him, I allowed my own eyes to react slightly. A subtle reaction of momentary confusion. It worked. His eyelids squinted a quarter of an inch from distracting thought over my unanticipated reaction. I had moved into him until we were only inches apart.

I pulled my six-shooter from my belt, jerking it out sideways, as I ran my left hand over the gun frame, fanning back the hammer while holding down the trigger. The gun clicked fired, as the barrel and muzzle of my gun was pushed into his belly. A draw done this way can be timed as taking half a second.

I know because I once had a neighbor who competed in fast draw like this and he showed me. Since I did not have to aim to hit anything, all I did was fan the hammer of the gun as I shoved it into his belly.

The eyes of the gunslinger no longer moved. They widened and froze. He never cleared leather. Like I show you in this book, he was thinking when he should have been just doing. I played him and broke his focus.

The Venus club was silent. I then polished him off by twirling the six-gun one revolution and spun it back into his holster. Just like in my tale, "15 Hours From Midnight," I kept saying loudly,

"You're good! You're really good!"

I left my opponent with as much dignity as possible. Some things in life are futile.

While I was walking off the stage, I could hear the enraged gunslinger behind my back, "Oh yeah!"

He was drawing his guns and shooting the back of my departing head. I could hear the clicks of the hammer falling.

"Oh yeah!"

Out of the corner of my eye, I spotted the masked wrestler chuckling sadistically; Mr. Hunter, was grinning in silent deep amusement.

I guess Venus is the only place that will let me be a cowboy.

LESSON LEARNED

In the moment of facing your opponent, never—ever—let yourself get distracted. It only takes the blink of an eye to lose the draw.

Distraction

We will define distraction as anything that takes your focus away from what you are doing. This will always momentarily occur, but if we dwell in distraction, then we cannot be our very best in what we do.

There can be physical distraction, such as stage lights in our eyes, uncomfortable clothing, illness, noise, temperature, and other people. These are external conditions under which we work. As annoying as these can be, we can minimize their effect on us through the commitment of complete focus.

It is the internal distractions that create the most harm to our performing at our best. Their appearance and existence can be much more tricky to determine. Though being "in a bad mode today" can lead to real distraction, it does not have the power of distraction in the mind. The list of mental distractions is a long one. So I will touch upon some of the most common in my observations. The actual order and occurrence of these is based on the individual's habits, such as:

- thinking too much
- unrealistic expectations
- self–editing
- directing while doing
- projecting into the future
- anticipating with a desire to control everything

We all think and know its value; I am referring to when thinking becomes a distraction while doing. Thinking is critical in preparing, making choices, and determining actions to do. But when the time comes to do; do with complete focus. Thinking will cause distraction, keeping you from full potential. I have seen this for the past thirty-four years of coaching acting.

For many, it can also paralyze doing. Too much thinking triggers hesitation, worry, doubt, and worst of all "freeze." It also removes connection with others and your relationships will suffer.

"When it's time to think—think."

"When it's time to do—do."

"But don't think while you are doing."

For those who still try to control,

"Don't think your way into right doing."

"Do your way into right thinking." This is called experience.

Expectations always lead to getting "thrown off." So many have this habit of delusion. Unless you have a magic crystal ball for telling fortunes, you will set yourself up for distraction and almost always disappointment. Should you have a habit of dwelling on expectations, here is a simple change of perspective for you:

Never expect anything

Never demand anything

Nothing is ever as I think it will be

Self-editing comes very easy to brilliant creative writers. Skill at self-editing is a tremendous accomplishment. However, doing this while you need to be simply doing, such as during speaking, will show up and create hesitation, worry, and doubt. If you self-edit while on-camera, we will see it in your eyes.

Directing is a part of great leadership. Sometimes it can slip into the darkness of control and micromanaging while performing or speaking. This can cause you to listen to yourself as you speak and there is a real distraction. If you do, and try to direct at the same time, you will usually come across as detached. Certainly, you cannot be wholehearted.

"What will the weather be like tomorrow?" calls for a projection. After all these years, how perfect is weather projection? It is about as perfect as waiting to begin my presentation while mentally projecting into the middle of it before I have even started. I have heard this admission a lot. In this book, I give you other things "to chew on" rather than the middle, before you even begin. Please "Keep your head where your feet are at."

Anticipating is similar to projecting but for our purposes, it is based more on "knowing the answers" or "knowing what will happen next." Anticipation kills the ability to appear spontaneous. Spontaneity is not knowing what will happen next. This is not chaos. Chaos has no form.

Your form is what you have worked on and prepared. That is not chaos—that is form. Spontaneity brings this to life and interest to others. Anticipation brings boredom to an audience from predictability.

Find some bad acting on TV. Viewers who talk to their TV will say,

"I bet he says_____."

Then the bad acting confirms the dialogue, causing, "see! I told you he'd say that."

The line about to be spoken was too predictable. Anticipated. Audience and performer have become detached.

What you say, whether lines in acting or keynote speech, should have the feeling of spontaneity. As if the speaker had never rehearsed and is creating the words as spoken naturally. In order to really succeed at this, you must have form. And you must know your form. Here is my term for spontaneity and improvisation:

- Freedom of movement

- Emotionally and physically

- Within a form
- The more free you appear—the more compelling you will be to others.

Being Business-like When a 9millimeter Comes to Call

I once had the business task of disarming a man with a 9mm Beretta pistol in his hand, as he approached the door. When the threat of disruption or hostile take-over approaches your door.

BUSINESS ADVICE

Move quickly—calmly—and surely. Stop him before he gets through your door.

Do not charge head-on into a reckless and costly direct approach. I moved along the plate glass windows, so that if fired upon, the hostile fire would likely deflect because of the shallow angle and interference between us. I moved with the indirect approach to his flank. Always use the indirect approach if possible.

BUSINESS ADVICE

Once you commit fully, never hesitate. The game will become new on it's own.

I surprised him. Once thrown off his game, I gave him no chance to think.

Face-to-face and eye-to-eye, I gave him a manner of escaping harm by holding out a basket to put his gun in, with no choice of when to disarm. If confused, they are afraid to take action. You make it seem like a good idea at the time.

My 45 pistol was on my right hip, holstered, but clearly handy for my right hand. Sometimes we need to show leverage to help encourage decisions.

My partner "in business" was so busy chatting to someone during this encounter, he had no idea of what had happened until after it was over.

LESSON LEARNED

In this real world,

"There are people like you who make things happen,

There are a lot people who things happen to,

And there are some people who don't know what happened."

How to Focus

For the ninety-nine percent of you who like power, focus is the key. This is so important to you I repeat our term focus is defined as –

"Doing one thing at a time fully with no distraction."

That means doing only one single action at a time, with absolutely nothing else going on mentally. It is momentary absolute commitment of self "with everything you've got."

Sounds hard? No. You have already done this in your life. Here are examples

Someone you know receives a note or letter or notification and you see this. You see them reading it. They become totally absorbed with the paper in their hands. It is as if nothing else exists except their involvement with the paper.

Doesn't that draw your total attention? For the moment, their complete focus draws your complete focus. That person, unaware of any distraction, becomes an attention magnet. You want to know what is going on with them.

Drawn to them, you carefully approach them, hoping they will awaken to your presence. Instead, your approach startles them and they jerk up gasping,

"Oh! I didn't see you!" or

"Oh! I didn't know you were here!"

What has happened is the other person was in full focus doing one thing, that temporarily shut out all else. They were lost in what they were doing.

Perhaps this simple experience or something similar has happened to you. If so, you have proven that you already have the ability to focus. You already have the ability to shut out distraction. Many have incorrectly convinced themselves that they cannot shut distraction out.

I enjoy cooking Italian food. It is a bit of a hobby with me and I have taken classes with chefs. I like garlic. My thoughts can falter to—if a little bit of garlic is good—then a lot of garlic must be great. However, if you overcook the garlic, it becomes a new bitter spice. The frying of garlic demands attention and I know that.

Being human, I like doing more things than just one at a time. Maybe I should have become a juggler. Who wants to do just one simple thing at a time. As the garlic fries in the olive oil, I somehow get involved in playing with the zucchini; or I obsess on the chopped flat parsley. I now, have once again, burned the delicate garlic. Distraction burns garlic and it also burns me.

Maybe this pitfall of a perspective comes from thinking I am a culinary juggler doing multi task deeds, when all I should be doing is simply frying the golden garlic. So much for "Aglio e Olio" linguine.

Focus is not normal in everyday life; but it is completely natural when we do not expect anything. Like when we admit, "I wasn't ready for that."

Because full-focus is rare in everyday life, those who see it are drawn to it. If you focus when you do things, it becomes a powerful people magnet to draw their full attention to you. To break this principle down; "Do one thing at a time fully!" Not only is it simple, it also empowers everything you do, especially through the interested eyes of others. If you only focus on breathing before you make an entrance, you will have no space in your mind in which to chew on yourself. The committee talking in your head will be pushed out to recess.

Imagine if you approach a stranger for a meeting and your intention is to help them. Fully focused, "meet and greet" them. Your actions will affect them in a compelling manner.

If your mind argues, "Well…my mind doesn't work that way."

Of course it doesn't. That is what I am saying. Because our minds can go all over the place, we have to subtract. We focus on one thing at a time. If this is done fully, distractions will leave because there is no longer space for them to sit.

If your mind still argues, "What if I have many things to do? What if I have many content points to make?"

You cannot make two powerful points at the same moment. It is amazing how many habitually think this way from complicating things in their life. You cannot say two words at exactly the same moment, though teens continue to try. You simply make one point at a time. Others will then clearly follow you. Help others to understand you. If you give us too much to chew on, you will give us enough to choke on.

Your clarity begins with yourself. Do one thing—at a time —fully.

Focus. You already have this power.

Follow Through – Never End Speaking

Long ago, in the long gone days of "phone booths," I was in my salad days in my beginning acting career. Here I was, on the uptown streets of New York, near the border of where things could get a "little hairy," minding my own business. I shut myself in a phone booth searching my pocket for some change to make a call. As I readied to punch in the phone number, from out of nowhere appeared a street troll.

He approached the glass of the phone booth and then pulled a knife. This ragamuffin had a good chance in placing first in the "who's your favorite psycho contest." True to troll form, he poked his knife at the glass near me and began to make really irritating scraping sounds with the blade. That cut it—I yelled,

"Knock it off! I'm on the phone!"

I then polished him off by staring at him the look of "how dare you interrupt me." I continued to silently gaze into his bloodshot eyes. This action is called follow through. Follow through with your eyes. Please note this term –

Follow through means—there is no such a thing as an ending —there is only the beginning of what happens next.

The street goblin turned into a glob. He sheepishly put his knife away and turned away like a hurt puppy. I watched him drag his feet away, down East 96th Street, leaving a trail of evil running down his leg.

I went back to punching in the phone numbers and soon found out that the phone was out-of-order. Sometimes in business or social encounters, confrontations turn out to be unnecessary.

The numero uno (Spanish) mistake that is made uno mas (my further cantina Spanish for "another drink"), that is to say the most common mistake of speakers, actors, talkers (both verbal and non-verbal) and most others on this planet is:

- Ending. With no follow-through.

Or

- Heard anyone's spoken words drop off at the end of speaking?
- Seen anyone's energy level take a dump as they end speaking?
- Seem to lose connection with others as they begin to finish speaking?
- Seen anyone's eyes go dead as they finish speaking?
- Slam their lips shut at the end of their speaking?
- Seem to weaken as they finish?

I could fill another book with symptoms you have seen or done. They all come from knowing or thinking that it is "the end." Knowing it is the end of a phrase, or thought, or sentence, or point, or speaking turn, or acting scene, etc.

I have written about the power of the "fear of the unknown." Not knowing in our minds. Thinking the delusion that it is more control to know as much as possible. This can slide into my own managing of knowing for sure when I am finishing speaking.

The huge problem becomes if I know I am ending speaking (perspective) and I then actually make my action ending speaking, then the consequences have to be just that. My anticipation of what will happen will cause me to "do end" prematurely. When this becomes normal, I will not even know that I am slamming things shut at the end. If fact, it will feel I am doing the right thing because I have chosen it to be a normal way of doing, harmfully thinking I can predict the end.

"A technique" of trying to swing the sound of my voice upward mechanically at the end of speaking will appear artificial because it is not ingrained within us.

The correction for this oh-so-common mistake in breaking connection at the end, both verbally and non-verbally, can be fixed right now with this simple change of perspective. There is no such thing as an ending; there is only the beginning of what happens next.

The action to do from this is: involve us with wanting to see what you will do next, even if we actually do not see this. We have the desire to go on and continue with you and what you are going to do. If we do not see you again, from wherever we left off, we will think of you and maybe even miss you (this is movie star quality).

Part of this is from your own sharing of feelings that follow through as if continuing and not abruptly ending. If you do not know it is over, we do not know it is over. This is what keeps you from "tailing off at the end."

You already know this. Pick up a favorite novel. When a chapter ended, it did not end for you. You wanted to see what happens next. If it is late and you need to get up in the morning, knowing what will happen next will cause you to give up the book. If you really want to find out (not knowing) what is next, you will not only stay with turning the next page, you will also stay up. Get your audience or others to want to turn your page.

If you like movies, what is a great movie to you? The scenes held you and you did not wish them to end. When they ended, you wanted to see what happens next. But bad performance will telegraph that it is the end and who cares what will follow.

Further proof is a sport. Is there follow through when swinging a golf club? Kicking a soccer ball? Shooting marbles?

How many trail away with your eyes as you finish saying your piece? Do you have a habit of that from previous relationships? I am not talking about a staring contest. I am not talking about being overly intense. But if you have something important to say and you maintain your eye contact for just a few moments after you speak, without dropping the end of your phrase, your relationship with them will change immediately. Try it and see what changes.

If I can do this with a street troll, you can do this with any of your own relationships, both personal and in business. Pay attention to great relationship scenes in books and movies. If you do not want to do that, just watch non-compelling people when they speak and see if you want that.

Instead of wanting to know what will happen—Experience the joy in finding and discovering it.

Then share that experience with us and never end—entice us with the beginning of what may happen next between us. Then we will have an interesting relationship.

Achieving That One-Hundred Percent

Whether my client is a high profile speaker or actor, most consider themselves to be "driven." So it is not surprising to be asked,

"How can I achieve being one hundred percent (100%)?"

I have seen this desire a lot. Once again, I give you a simple solution that will work for you with this driven wish.

First, when I was driven, if I felt that I had achieved 100%, I did not stay satisfied for long. I felt restless. What else is there? What is next?

A person who is driven would prefer the results to be from their own making. I will raise and make myself reach that elusive 100%. If I do this, how much will it take for me? After all, I am an over-achiever. Unfortunately, 101% becomes overdone and I am now too much, especially to other people.

I believe that consistency is more important than 100%. It is better for you to be 90% to 80% consistent, than to be 98% sometimes but 45% other times. If you are 90% to 80%, you are a pro. You are also very good to excellent! If you remain that consistent, you will gain full confidence.

Full confidence is how you will be moved to 95%. You will not get there by pushing, forcing, or self-will. Tried and true confidence is the way to the final 10%.

"So how about the last elusive 5% to achieve a full 100%?"

From thirty-four years of teaching acting and speaking, here is your solution:

"You always achieve the final 5% of 100%—by doing nothing."

Please consider, "Inside all of us, there is a part that we hold back (habit). This part, hidden in the depth of our heart, is the part that must never be stepped on, spit on, or laughed at. It is our fragile essence and is protected from all harm. This unique part of us, can be held out at times in our life, but it may be only rarely given. Some may never hold out the best part of themselves."

You may ask, "Am I supposed to talk about this to everyone?"

"No. Then it would lose it's special power. What you do is you give yourself freely, while not holding back. When you give all of you, by doing nothing to hold back, you will be the very best you can be. Though not normal, this is completely natural. This part of ourselves that we hold back is truly our gold. Give and share your gold and others will admire you for this freedom, faith, and courage. You will have what they want" and are giving of it freely."

One Hundred Percent. Wholeheartedly.

After Dark in The Everglades

To describe the Everglades as a natural tropic region in South Florida is like saying a shark is a big fish that prefers a paleo diet. The description leaves out the feeling "danger." This mysterious jungle within the U.S., harbors deadly alligators and crocodiles, toxic snakes both crawling and two legged, and flying bugs practicing for the end times.

So before we begin another of my little adventures, please close your eyes for a moment and imagine yourself, after dark, alone, in the middle of the Everglades. Your imagination will set our stage.

It all began with a gold plated 158 grain lead round nose 38 special bullet. I should have taken this as a sign of what will come. This gold plated bullet was attached to a big gaudy man's gold plated necklace chain. The kind of big flashy gold man's necklace that sophisticated women move away from.

This same gold plated bullet necklace was hung around the neck of a Cuban man, who looked like he was costumed for a drug movie. He wore a "wife beater" sleeveless underwear t-shirt that was covered with an open tropical shirt, printed with big palm trees and the saturated colors of happy birthday gift wrapping.

To top this costume off literally was a white small brim straw hat.

I did not look directly at him, as he moved down the plane aisle, canvassing for the safest place to sit. He stopped next to me. I would not want to miss this golden opportunity, so I grinned (relationship) and motioned (gesture) for him to "Please have a seat."

We were aboard a World War II restored B-24 bomber. This cool flight leaves from Miami and flies low level over the top of The Everglades. What a great view from this grand old propeller driven bomber.

As we flew over the South Florida jungle, my Cuban neighbor was silent. That means jail. I could tell he had no interest in looking out the window during this incredible flight. That means he was local and familiar with the run of this airplane. Since he would not begin a conversation, I decided to open up the ball and considered how to break the ice. Would it be?

"I can't help but notice_____." No. That's much too corny.

How about, "That is quite a _____." No. He's Cuban, not British.

"Hey man" No. Too familiar. He might think I'm making a pass at him. In this type of business encounter, one must be brief, leading, and get the other person to want to brag. It also helps to make him think he is smarter than me. So I went with a bit of awe, "That's some necklace."

My new campadre measured my sincerity and then broke into a smile. True to form, his front teeth were also gold plated. He was like a walking hedge fund against inflation. The Cuban became an ambassador of good will and bragged,

"Yeah man. Dey dug eet outta' me." Flash of gold teeth.

I followed up with a relationship feeling of happy and friendly,

"It's good for you that's all they dug."

After a moment of contemplating me, the gold plated teeth screamed laughter. I wasn't that funny, but it is nice to perpetuate joy to the world.

It was in the early 1980's and I was on a brief vacation that I chose to ruin by researching drug running in South Florida. In Hollywood, I had a screenplay I wrote being considered by an agent to give to one of his stars, who had a network development money deal for producing a TV series pilot. So I got the bright idea of how drugs could be smuggled into the mainland U.S. via The Everglades. I would use my investigative and undercover skills to find out the skinny of how drugs were really brought in.

My newfound Cuban friend would only carefully reveal to me how big the drug smuggling business was in Florida and how dangerous it was with the involvement of so many amateurs. With the exception of how much he loved eating black beans, he was very cautious in what he revealed to me. I guess he did not want to increase the gold plated bullet to a pair.

After I reached my destination, I made a survey feeling out the area. I will leave out a lot of the footwork and just boil it down to;

Underneath the area's beauty, something was wrong. Not spoken about and kept silent.

In a difficult economy, some businesses seemed to be thriving.

Outside of the small retirement town, there was a lot of poverty, clearly houses and yards of the poor.

However, I noticed some of these houses and yards of poverty would also have some expensive child's toys strewn about, like rich kids might toss their toys around.

The local fishermen with old boats had strange behavior, especially for people regulated into business difficulty, forcing poverty upon them.

So it struck me. Who would know The Everglades better than the salty poor locals, especially, the poor fishermen.

There were also numerous small hidden dirt roads in the depth of The Everglades that a small plane could land on.

If I was to run drugs into this area, I would buy locals who were bitter anyway at the government and its rules. Once in The Everglades, knowing the in's and out's of the jungle, who would catch them? Especially…after dark. If they were caught, they could just dump the goods. No finer drug mules could be found at any cash price. The fishing boats, navigated by locals, could run circles around the Feds.

Armed with this research, I now needed to confirm with corroborating evidence. I chose a small gun shop to begin.

I guessed the slowest time for this small gun shop would be a weekend morning. Maybe the owners would be out shooting or nursing a hang over.

At 10:00am, the bell above the door tinkled, as I entered the empty shop. A young man in his latter teens came out of the back room and moved behind the counter of handguns. He tried to act older and wiser,

"Help you?"

I heard no other noise and seemed to be in luck. This young man would be cautious and guarded with a stranger in the empty gun shop.

I looked around with the best stupid naïve look on my face that I could manage. I then greeted him with my eyes and began to break the ice,

"I've never been in a Florida gun store. I'm from California."

He nodded to my lead with something in common, "I was there once. Disneyland."

"That's exactly where I'm from. L.A."

"They got big gun stores in L.A."

"Yeah. But this is really nice. People aren't so nasty here."

He smiled friendly and the ice was broken. We began to talk. He was alone and "in charge", opening the store this morning. He became a bit cocky and the two of us promoted him to being an expert on firearms. I gave him a PhD. I let it slip,

"I want to see the Everglades. But I heard it could be dangerous…and not from alligators."

"Huh. You can wind up with your legs cut off and fed to the sharks. They'll be nothing left of you to find."

Our talk confirmed my research. The drugs were being run through the south Everglades. Because they were amateurs, bags of drugs were tossed into the waters, when the boat runners got scared bad enough. Suitcases of cash were the rewards; because most were not career criminals, they had no idea of laundering money. So mattresses were stuffed to capacity and cans of money were buried all over the yards.

Then we evolved into pay dirt. The young man offered to show me around a bit. I would meet him at the shop in two days, on his day off, for the inside tour. We bid a friendly "so long."

The next day, I attempted to get some information from the local paper. I was given the editor on the phone. I did not want the editor and I did not ask for him. He began by screaming at me. I did nothing to deserve this yelling tirade about leaving things alone and he ended with;

"You know. People have been killed for asking too many questions."

Our chat ended with him slamming the phone in my ear. Interesting editor.

Many seem to think that drugs only involve users and criminals. Consider who else would get involved with an influx of cash. How about the very legitimate citizens and businesses selling expensive air boats or new cars or guns or motorcycles or aircraft? What if a former poverty struck person knew nothing about what to do with a lot of cash, especially if they thought the Cayman Islands were a part of Hawaii. Does money spread to "non criminals?"

I am not saying that every boat or plane owner ran drugs; but there may have been a few who fell to temptation. Especially when the mattress was full.

The bell over the door of the small gun shop tinkled once more. Everything looked the same except for one glowing change. The young cocky man who was to be my tour guide was transformed and I don't mean with a glow.

I could smell it. His eyes betrayed him. No longer was he loose mouthed. He was cautious and spoke a bit too casual,

"Hey. Ready for your tour."

I bounced back, "You ready?"

"Oh. I can't go anymore. Something came up. But I got a friend to show you around."

"What friend?"

"Oh. Well. He's gonna' meet you at the pier."

"The pier?"

"Yeah. At 10:00pm tonight."

I felt like asking for a mirror so that I could see how stupid I must look. My acting experience rated his performance at four thumbs down. I was too busy to be a critic, inching my way towards the door.

"Great. I'll have to call you later. I didn't expect tonight."

"I'll be here 'til six."

"Talk to you later...and thanks."

The bell above the door tinkled again, as I made it out the door. The air always smells good after you make an escape in one piece.

Part of the purpose of this little vacation was to visit a well-retired man. He spent his whole life working hard, owning a furniture store in Ft. Wayne, Indiana. Like many in the upper mid-west, he dreamed of someday retiring to warm sunny Florida and playing golf, vowing never to wear a tie again. I had been keeping him posted on my little adventure and then told him of being "set-up" with the meeting on the pier. This silver haired sun tanned man quietly and solemnly promised,

"I'll go with you."

That really hit me. Here is a man in his late 70s willing to "go with me." A man who only wants peace in the twilight of his life. A man who plays golf six times a week, reads the Wall Street Journal as a conservative follower of "The Intelligent Investor", and is in bed by 8:00pm. A man who was willing to walk towards danger.

Then I remembered that he served as a navy lieutenant on a destroyer ship during World War II. One of his fondest memories of youth was being put up in uniform, by courtesy, at the Waldorf-Astoria hotel before he was to ship out . Here is an old fashioned stand up WWII Vet still with quiet courage. I have great respect for that generation and their fidelity.

But it was time to exit. I could always run for it, but he lived there in peace. If they were to get me, they would get him too. It was time to climb aboard that old B-24 bomber and fly off into the "sky blue yonder." It took what it took, but I really began to see how my own self-will could have real consequences for others.

LESSON LEARNED

My own perspective frames how I treat others, especially the people I love and care about. Consequences of my actions do not end with me.

The Narrow Road to Joy Is Deeply Paved with Pain

Colossians 4:6 "Let your speech be always with Grace, seasoned with salt, that you may know how you ought to answer each one."

Recovery is Getting Back What I Once Lost

If it is so simple and do-able to achieve the very best I can be, then what happened to me? I need to walk the talk and tell you the truth.

My problems were rooted from my past. The most powerful demons were the ones I refused to look at, even though they were in plain sight in between my ears. Those demons came to life from my childhood and youth. How can it be possible that what happened in my childhood and teens could forge so many undesirable results in my life...twenty, forty, sixty years later? Look at how much self-will I ran with. For me, the years of "growing up" hold the keys to me, my adult life, and its pain.

I am neither a doctor nor a psychiatrist. I invite you to judge me. I invite you to analyze me. My story is the truth. I no longer have the luxury of lying.

I was born in 1948 in Chicago. To be exact, South Side Chicago. What does that have to do with later causing my adult self-will to ruin my perceptions of myself and others? It had plenty to do with it.

1948 was only a few painful years of recovery after the end of WWII. My parents were both second generation Japanese-Americans, who had never been outside of the US. But they ended up in Chicago as a result of the WWII relocation of Japanese Americans from the pacific coast to internment camps in the mid-west in 1942. My mother was sent to a barbed wired internment camp at Heart Mountain, Wyoming and my father was sent to Arkansas. So after they married, my parents ended up living in Chicago.

After I turned one year old, my mother brought me back to California by airplane. She told me later in life that no one would help her on the trip, even with me crying and having fits regularly. At one point, she held me and just sat down and cried.

Generally speaking, the second generation Japanese-Americans were known to be quiet, hard working, and law abiding. Like many other ethnic groups, they sacrificed their lives to give their children a better chance at life.

I believe almost all people suffer from discrimination in one form or another. How does this reality affect our perspectives and our personalities.

In those days of the 40's and 50's, a lot of people took a lot of black and white pictures with "brownie" cameras and flashcubes. If you were to look at my childhood photos up to five years of age, you would see a happy carefree goofy show-off kid. If you look at my pictures after I started kindergarten, you will see a different child. The smile went away and my head progressively goes down with each year of school.

When first exposed to the world, I found out that I had started WWII and then the Korean war. I began to shut down. My wonderful sympathetic kindergarten teacher told my mother; "He seems to want to express himself—but he is afraid to and can't."

As I grew into becoming a boy, things got much worse. A trusted friend could turn on me in a moment and leave me with hurt feelings. So I learned not to trust. I became hyper-sensitive but hid my feelings. To avoid pain, I became hyper-vigilant, always watching for trouble around me.

When you get surrounded by a bunch of guys, you can't fight everybody. So I learned how to manipulate and play others. If picked-on physically, I learned you can get knocked down but never give in and cry "uncle." Never surrender. Just get back at them later in revenge.

Girls were out of the question. Imagine what their parents would say if I showed up at the door. So girls became associated with pain and distance. This did not go away by itself in later adult relationships. Intimacy remained fearful.

The shame, fear, not fitting in, not feeling a part of, was setting the stage in Act I of my life. My play shifted from setting light-hearted romantic comedy to dark brooding tragedy.

To put it in a nutshell, my story was "I never wanted to be me." Talk about being powerless over something leading to life being a dilemma. This perspective created habitual behavior of hiding in the middle. I became driven to being the class clown. I was the invisible friend to girls who were having troubles with other boys. I was safe being detached. I believed in buying friends. I felt like a coward.

In high school, I found acting. I found the perfect place to hide. I could be admired for not being me. What I did not know is there is a difference between amateur acting and professional acting. Professional acting is about being believable and using your own self emotionally. I made the mistake of a coward choosing a battlefield to hide out in. It was time to meet my friend. I found alcohol. Here was another place to hide and escape. It started out with my buddies and me, drinking six packs of beer to have fun and get "out of it." After drinking, we became bigger, taller, better looking, as our insecurity was thrown up in the bushes.

I did not like the taste of alcohol at first, but I sure liked the effect.

From the gate, I was not a social drinker. I wanted to get drunk and shut my head off and forget my hidden fears.

When I turned twenty-one years old, I was on the rifle range at Ft. Lewis. After I left basic training, my buddies and I headed straight for the airport bar. Like many others, I began to drink alcoholically while in the service.

For the next twenty years, I became a drunk. As you can tell from my tales, I was always functional, but I was progressively heading down towards a bottom. I was in the worst relationship of my life—my relationship with me. When you reach the point of no longer wanting to live with yourself, there are but few options left.

The drinking that started out as so much fun—turned into not so much fun and problems—then crossed the line of becoming nothing but problems.

I could stop drinking for a while, but I could not quit no matter what. I was making more money than I had ever made in my life, before or since. I was attempting big business deals. I was acting on television and in movies. Which all brings about a huge difficulty besides denial. It is so hard to walk away. It is even harder to walk away from perceived material "success."

There is a famous empty hole inside. We can try to fill it with alcohol, drugs, money, power, property, and prestige, but it never works. The wind still blows completely through it. I was trying to fill the hole with the wrong spirit.

Finally, one night my heart broke. I was still breathing but I died inside. It takes pain to die into a new life. For each individual, it takes what it takes. For me, it took the death of self.

So twenty-eight years ago, I began a program of recovery that was not of my own making. One day at a time, I have not had a drink for over twenty-eight years. It is clear now that I was hopeless. Today, except for a hospital stay and the usual array of health issues from birthdays, I am in much better health than when I was twenty-five years old and drunk.

From hindsight, I now see that I did not begin recovery to get sober. I would have told you that, but at that point, I lied so much that I became "honest in my lying." I had no sense of the truth from the false. I probably came into recovery as an arrogant self-centered act to stop my problems. It matters not what my motives were at that time. What matters is that I made a commitment to do what I did not want to do, but did it anyway.

Everything about the program of recovery went against my grain. It was in direct opposition to my past. After my childhood, how could I trust and let go? In business, if I don't move the rock myself then who will? It won't get moved. So I have to do it myself.

This began with admitting that I was the problem and the problem cannot fix the problem. But that is the obsession. I am not telling you to do this. That is entirely up to you. But I needed help so this is what I did.

I had to make a written inventory of what my wrongs were. What I did that was a wrong does not mean the other person is right or was right. It does not even mean that I did something bad to them. It is a written admission that something inside me was wrong such as; was I running from self-centered fear or was I not being honest with myself and others. It is a list of my harms concerning others.

It didn't take long before a pattern emerged. A repeating pattern (habitual behavior) that plays over and over like an old broken record. Faced with my repeated actions on paper, as opposed to how things can change in the mind, I became sick of it all. No matter how long I stared at the writing, it wouldn't change. This began the journey of looking at myself, which drinking gave me an escape.

I then took my inventory and shared it with a trusted person in confidence. Choose well someone you really can trust. The important thing is that you admit everything verbally and get it out destroying the power of the secret.

This one simple but difficult action will change your entire life, if you are honest about it. Who can go to this length? We all can if we are willing.

I then turned all of my shortcomings and defects of character over to a God, whom at that time I had no understanding of, or experience with, on a conscious level.

My inventory made a list of all persons I had harmed. I set about to make amends to them personally and face-to-face, wherever possible. This is not an apology and it is not seeking forgiveness. It is not unusual to get thrown out or told off as a result. It is to take care of my side of the street. I do not harp directly on what I did. That would just cause further pain and harm. I only express my wrongs in terms of my own selfishness, self-seeking, dishonesty (with them or me), inconsiderate thoughts or actions, or fear driven behavior. An experienced advisor, caring but detached from the situations is of great help.

This will take time. From my original list of persons I had harmed, there is only one left outstanding. If I were to run into her, I am entirely willing to make amends, right then and there.

Right about now, this procedure is not sounding too appetizing. Easily, any mind can go to work, "Well that's fine for alcoholics and addicts. But I am not one of them." What does this have to do with me?"

So here is a true tale of a non-alcoholic "normie" who worked in the mainstream of business.

I was once asked to help a lady, who was right on the verge of giving up her career. She worked for one of the largest business conglomerates in the U.S. This mid- thirties businesswoman was very good at her job and looked forward to a future with her large company.

The problem was that her supervisor at the company did everything she could to make life and work miserable for this lady. This mistreatment was done in a constant deliberate manner to either get this victim fired or force her to quit.

Rather than quitting from the anxiety, this lady fought to keep her job. She really wanted to stay with the company and was afraid of the lack of security of leaving. She admitted the fear of going through the upcoming freezing winter without a job. Her dream was to get married and have a child.

Having exhausted all means to resolve this problem, she was willing to go to any lengths for a solution. She asked for my help and promised to follow any directions I may have for her.

She took a much needed one-week vacation from back east to California. This lady was in no way an alcoholic or an addict. She was as normal as normal can be. But she was beaten to a pulp from her supervisor at work, who also carried the abuse to outside of the office. In this case, her supervisor was a woman.

We met face-to-face. She was done fighting. She surrendered to win.

We then started a written inventory of what wrongs were going on inside her. At that point, I heard a too familiar reply,

"What! I didn't do anything wrong to her. She's the one!"

That was my familiar cue, "I didn't say you did wrong things to her. I mean where were your wrongs?"

"What? It was her."

"Were you ever dishonest?"

"I never lied to her."

"Were you always honest with yourself?"

She was thrown into silence. I tried to look intelligent.

Shakespeare wrote, "Above all, to thine own self be true."

More silence. That usually precedes either the truth or violence. So softly,

"Were you honest with yourself?"

Her eyes began to get moist. She looked at me and shook her head. I eased into sharing,

"If I am in denial, I am lying to myself. Denial is when I rationalize or justify or excuse what I do. If none of those do the trick, then I can always blame. All of these will harm me."

Her face and her body and her feelings, sank into a release. I said into her hurt eyes,

"I am not above this—I am in the middle of it."

She was now ready and so was I,

"Were you consumed with yourself?"

"Maybe you became self-seeking."

"Were you inconsiderate? Even to yourself?"

I leaned my eyes towards her,

"Were you running on fear?"

The dam broke. It broke because it always wanted to break. At this time, I never interfere when this happens. It is no longer between them and me. She finally spoke in sobs,

"I'm scared. I don't want to be pushed out of my job. I worked hard for it. But I can't take anymore."

I let her get to her fear. After she caught her breath,

"What if I end up alone and freezing this winter."

This will lead to her fear list, which will lead to the "Key" to the real fears. To uncover the key to the fear, I use three questions to get to the core of the truth.

Here is an example (not from this same lady):

Question 1 "What are you afraid of?"

Answer 1 "Being broke."

Question 2 "Why are you afraid of being broke?"

Answer 2 "I won't have any money."

Here is where some searches stop. Here is where we really begin. Answer2 is not the answer. It is the dependency or symptom. To find the root of the problem we need what was not said,

Question 3 "So you don't have any money—now what are you really afraid of?"

I now need to shut up and listen. Sometimes the most spiritual thing to do is to shut up. You will often see blockage (habitual behavior),

Answer 3 avoided "I told you. I…uh…what do you mean?"

Question 3 deeper "What are you really afraid of?"

Don't stop digging until you feel the truth from inside the person. It will not be about "money" or something outside of the person. It will be from the fragileness within their heart. A few examples could be:

"That my Father was right. I will never amount to anything."

Or, "I don't deserve anything."

Or, "I'll never be good enough—no matter what I do."

The key is always the lie. It is the incorrect perspective from before. Remember our word perspective? It is at the height of its power when kept a secret. It is possible for the person not to realize or even be aware of this. We may have no clue. Or it can be so important, that it was minimized for a lifetime to become disguised as "no big deal."

When the truth comes to light, I have seen an awakening in the eyes that cannot be described in words. It is a divine moment of clarity. It is true freedom. And the price tag is always pain.

The worst pains I have gone through in my life have been the greatest gifts. I just didn't like the way the gifts were wrapped. I spent the first half of my life avoiding the pain and truth through drinking. The first battle is over the alcohol, but the lifetime war for most of us is over power.

Back to our courageous businesswoman. From the inventory and the admission with her mouth, she accepted and owned it all. Do not ever think that she liked any of this. This will never be a fit.

So now came the kiss of death. I let her know that she was to make a face-to-face amends to her supervisor, admitting only her own wrongs. She cannot bring up anything about her supervisor. There will be no blow-by-blow details and no desire for forgiveness or acknowledgement of being right at any time. All she can do is admit her own wrongs without harming her supervisor.

After I told all of this to our lady, I thought she was going to throw up on me. She stared at me in disbelief and whispered,

"Are you crazy?"

The emotional resistance for non-alcoholics is way more than for the self-loathing alcoholic. Without self-punishing guilt, a healthy person actually has a harder time with this amends. Then our lady was given help from her angel.

Remember that our lady had only taken a one-week vacation. She deserved this brief break after working insane amounts of hours and no time off. So what does her supervisor do? She calls long distance,

"I am flying to San Francisco airport. I know you are on vacation but you need to meet me. I will meet with you for one hour at the airport. Tomorrow."

How is that for habitual abusive behavior? What a gift! Thank God.

I think that this added bonus threw our lady into so much shock that she saw this was meant to be.

She drove up to San Francisco airport for her bogus meeting and soon to be divine appointment for making her amends.

At the airport, she met her supervisor and at the end of their meeting made her direct amends. The supervisor was speechless. She could only mumble,

"I see. I see."

If one is going to "eat crow," it goes down smoother while it is still warm.

The supervisor fell into toxic shock and our courageous lady was now free. She told me of how beautiful the drive was returning home.

From that moment on, her life changed completely.

One week after our lady returned to work, the supervisor stuck her in the back harder. The difference was—it lost its power. There is nothing more frightening to an abuser than when they push your buttons and the buttons no longer work. After losing her hostage, the supervisor pulled all stops to attack her victim. So much so, that the supervisors of this supervisor noted her dysfunctional behavior, cutting her own throat.

Eventually our lady left the company on her own and in good standing. I talked with her in the depth of the freezing winter. She was by herself in her cold apartment but she was happy. I don't mean feeling good. I mean she had a joy and peace, being set free with the truth.

A far better job came along and she got the new job. She met a man—got married—and the last I heard, she had a baby.

All I did was share my experience, strength and hope and never leave her when she wanted to cut and run. My own lifetime of mistakes was my gift to her. The worst of me was used for the good. She helped me more than I ever could help her. That is the power demonstrated through people.

In the past twenty-eight years of not taking a drink, during which I have hit three bottoms worse than anything while I was drunk. Pain hurts much more when you can't pass out in the gutter anymore. But the lesson is always on the other side of the pain. When you peel your onion, the tears always come.

If I examine my perspective and then change my actions from what I habitually did before, it is impossible for the results and consequences to be the same.

If I can do it—so can you.

My Testimony

In 1981, I was invited by a major publishing company to write a book on acting. I am grateful that I did not write at that time. I was not ready.

I now write out of the depth of Act III of my life. From my past told in the tales, I am still alive for a reason and that is the mission of this book. In recovery, our stories touch upon what we were like, what happened, and what we are like now. This chapter is simply what happened to me. I tell you the truth in testimony.

As you have read, I am a third generation Japanese-American. My parents wanted to assimilate, so the religious culture they inherited of Buddhism was only kept in tradition and to honor their parents. For my religion, funerals were held at the Buddhist temple and that was about it.

After my mother passed away, my sisters and I were going through her old documents and found a government card she had filled out upon entrance to the relocation center she was sent to during WWII. She listed on this registration card that she was "Christian." We were never told about this by my mother.

As a kid, I had a neighbor whose culture was from the migration from Oklahoma to California during the 1930's. My friend had a large family living in a tiny cottage and usually ate a lot of beans cooked in bacon. But he had these cool colored beads and really neat little cartoon booklets from the Catholic church. So I wanted to become Catholic. That did not fly with my father.

In elementary school, every Thursday afternoon was dedicated to "religious education." The Christian kids got to leave school and walk in a group to a church two blocks away. Those kids got to pray (whatever that was) and I had to do boring school work with the other kids left behind in the classroom.

Left behind? So I decided to try to get out of Thursday afternoon school by becoming a Christian. That did not fly either.

When I was thirteen years old, I had a Jewish friend. He was given a Barmitzvah, where he got all of this money, just for turning thirteen. Why can't I be Jewish? Well, that really didn't fly also.

As you have read, I enlisted in the army at a very hazardous time. We were given two "dog tags" to always wear around out neck. These were used to identify us should harm come, as in "killed in action." The metal tags were stamped with name, service number, and blood type for emergency transfusion (which mine was incorrect). There was also stamped "Religious Preference" and mine read "No Preference." I remember at that time saying,

"If it comes to that, what's the difference anyway."

So I spent the next twenty years drunk. Drunk alcoholics do not follow God. We are too busy playing God. The only spirits needed to fill the empty hole in my heart was of the liquid type. The word "spirit" has a number of definitions, one of which has to do with the highest form of experience with God and the other definition is "a deadly poison."

As the process of recovery from alcoholism took hold, my closed door to God, any god, was opened about a half-an-inch. Let's just say my door's deadbolts were unlocked.

I could not even say the term "higher power" in exchange for the word "God." I began with saying, "a power other than me."

When I was a kid, I had some kind of idea of a God, usually from punishment. Some kids could get away with doing wrong. Not me, I always got caught or ended up paying for it in some way or another. When I did wrong deliberately, I knew in my heart that I would "get it" sooner or later.

Throwing myself fully into recovery, I listened to others share their stories. It did not take long before I gave up the idea that they were all liars. After listening to hundreds of alcoholics in recovery, there emerged a couple of common threads, besides what a friend's little granddaughter observed,

"They say God and cuss in the same sentence."

In the beginning, I identified with people who were "angry at God" or anyone who was angry at anything. What I could not understand in all my brilliance was how some of these drunks got sober. Some were so bad and worse than I ever was. I had no answer to how these hopeless cases stopped drinking and were still alive.

I like a child's definition of the word "miracle,"

"A miracle is something that can't happen—but does."

I began to have my eyes and ears opened and saw an endless supply of living miracles. For someone like me, who lived by my wits and survived so many dangerous situations, becoming negative, skeptical, and knowing all; this really pulled my covers.

After about six months of being sober, I began to get my feelings back. It took that long. I remember a carpenter friend from Germany sharing that he was diagnosed with a severe cancer. Finally, I felt something in my heart that was not selfish. By the way, this German carpenter went into remission and is still alive today. Miracle.

Some people seem to go to church to find a miracle. I was surrounded by miracles but had no grasp of the reasons for them. In this seemingly backwards manner, I started to develop faith.

I was asked privately many times by others to visit their church, but I always had plenty of good excuses of why I couldn't go. Church was fine for them, but it was not for me.

After years of white washing the "god issue", I finally accepted that there was a God, but I had no clue of what that meant or was. Looking back, I still wanted to maintain my delusion of power, "doing God's will—my way."

If an agnostic is one who is incapable of knowing, that was me. Whatever you want to believe is up to you, just don't lay it on me.

But as the years of helping others (love?) added up, my closed door began to open up a bit more. It was through changed relationships with others, that I began to change. Our deepest healing comes with those we used to hate. I also had to learn to forgive, including forgiving myself. This was the most difficult trial in sobriety. I finally was awakened to the realization that I did not want to forgive myself. I did not want to give up the power of self-punishment.

All my life I have been driven. I was driven to prove myself, from what I went through as a youth. I reached a sober point in my life where I stopped long enough to ask myself, "What was I driven to prove?" I never took the honest time to look at that. I spent half my life trying to prove myself. Why?

It gives me joy to report that to this day, I do not have a true answer to why I was so driven. I never really knew why I had to prove myself. All of the damage that my self-will caused had no true and conscious reason.

During sixteen years of working on new ways of looking at things (perspectives) and new ways of doing (actions) instead of the old ways of self (habits), I had hit two major bottoms in sobriety that caused me to experience two living spiritual experiences, with no rational explanations. The pain of those bottoms were two of the greatest gifts of my life. I was leveled by God both times.

And then I met a woman.

After two failed marriages, I was hesitant about getting into another relationship. Not only that, but she was also in recovery. I had sworn off of any alcoholic women, drunk or sober. Especially one, who was going through another divorce herself. She resisted also. The bond of two people with that much baggage can really add fuel to the fire. An explosion that makes no sense. When the smoke cleared, we ended up together.

The image of love is wonderful. But the reality of love in this flesh may not be a possibility. To meet "the right one" is what dreams are made of. But reality may not cooperate with the dream.

Our old friend time has such an effect on us. I can meet the right one, but if the time is not right also, then it may not work. If I meet the right one—too soon—or too late—then tragically love may not be enough.

I have almost died a number of times. The one thing that I have experienced every time on the verge of death—is the absence of time. Everything slows down to only one moment. That one moment, with no time past and no time to come, always brings complete peace. When there is no time, there is absolute peace.

Andrea and I could not be together in this life. Neither of us had the power to make it. We were going to get married. We failed and separated.

Just before Christmas 2007, I got a phone call. Andrea died.

One more time in my life, I died.

I got rid of my job, took off my gun, and was done. All I could do was pray to dream about her. I began to hope that I would see her again.

We placed Andrea's ashes at the ocean side south of Santa Cruz, California, as she requested. I would go sit on a bench under the scent of tall eucalyptus trees on a steep cliff overlooking the Monterey bay. On a clear day, I could see a crystal blue ocean that seemed to have no end. I would be drawn there four to five times a week. I always brought flowers.

When there is death, I first think about what I was like and said to the person the last time I had contact with them. That is quite a lesson. The last time Andrea and I spoke, she was yelling at me. None of that mattered anymore. I just wished I would have replied, "I love you." That is all that matters. She used to ask me three times in a row, "Do you love me?"

So I drove the thirty miles to sit by the ocean breeze. I knew that Andrea loved Jesus and he was her Lord. I was ignorant on what it took to get into heaven or who Jesus really was. Once, Andrea was being wheeled into surgery and she sat up on the gurney, with a goofy smile on her face and promised me,

"If I die—I'll wait for you in Heaven."

I was just hoping that she made it there. So I began to say little prayers for her. In recovery, I was introduced to prayer. Though I was sober from a hopeless state, I would say, "spirituality was the weakest part of my program." That is how much I missed the point. When I first tried prayer, I felt uncomfortable and stupid.

I was like a lot of others. I had just enough honesty to get by and just enough prayer to ward off disaster. But my heart was not in it. I still held back that one hundred percent of myself. I did not give myself wholeheartedly.

On that cliff overlooking the endless sea, I began to really mean my intercessory prayers for Andrea. But instead of feeling full, I felt more empty.

It was the most beautiful day of my life, bright and sunny with a gentle ocean breeze blowing sparkles across the blue waters of the bay. I looked out at the horizon and I was completely empty. I let go of all self. Nothing left. A wholeness of peace came over me sitting on the bench at the top of the cliff.

I was done. The sky above was no longer at a distance; it was within reach. I looked up in quiet joy,

"Lord. It's a beautiful day. It's a beautiful time to take me."

I meant this with all of my heart,

"I'm ready. I'm done. I beg you. Please take me now."

I asked for death—He gave me life.

There was a still moment and then I felt peace. I was still breathing but I died.

As I drove back over the hills, I knew where to go next. A friend had been asking me if I wanted to meet her at the church she attended. She also happened to previously rent the same room that Andrea died in. I promised her that I would meet her next Sunday at the doorsteps of her church.

For my sixty years of ripping and running and running and gunning, I had only walked into a church for a wedding or a funeral. I was not used to any of this.

When I first walked into her church, I looked for someone to relate to. Of course, when you do that, all you see is differences. In the sanctuary, I spotted a shaved headed man who looked like he could bench press five hundred pounds. He had a communication speaker device on, so I decided that he was the bouncer. He looked like he could be a "NY door guy." I broke my silence with my friend,

"Is that guy the church bouncer?"

She made a wrinkled face and tossed a look at me,

"No. He's the Senior Pastor."

So much for church. Next, I did not like all of the singing. However, when the music changed to a hymn, I began to cry. It was a sudden release and I was moved emotionally by the music.

Had that Senior Pastor preached "fire and brimstone" or if everyone rolled around on the floor, I would have bolted out of there. Instead, "the bouncer" shared honestly and openly, like I was used to from the recovery program. He even admitted things and made it clear that this was about "a relationship not a religion." He got my attention when he referred to people who were there checking out and "kicking the tires." At the end, he invited new comers to meet him after the service.

I became emotional as I walked up to the Pastor and his wife. He sure must have spotted me coming. He reacted with immediacy as I approached him. He was preparing a piece of paper as I stopped in front of him. He introduced himself and his wife. He could read my pain,

"I want you to call me…right away…I would like to meet with you."

At our first meeting, I had a lot of questions. So I volunteered to read the entire Bible and would then set up another meeting with him. I liked the man.

Being an overachiever, I spent hours each day reading the Bible, as fast as I could, from Genesis to Revelation. After I finished, I made another appointment. At that meeting, I held up the Bible to this Senior Pastor and let go,

"If I am understanding any of this at all—then this is the most important meeting of my life."

Pastor glowed. He never forgot that and held me to it. He gave me a modern translation study Bible and I began a new life. It only took me sixty years of pain. For some of us—it takes—what it takes.

I have come within a thin hair of death by drowning twice (once when drunk and once when crazy). I like things happening in three's. I always said that the third time water would get me and I would die. I was baptized in water.

The great depression of 2008 and 2009 hit me deeply. For the first time in the old or the new life, I was in desperate financial trouble. The thought of me going bankrupt had never crossed my mind. I was $60,000 in hard debt and floating 0% APR checks to postpone what a SCORE business advisor had evaluated me, "You are doomed."

My credit was shot and fading away quickly. I inventoried my finances and I was done. Done again.

So I went for a walk in this new life with God. I walked by a deep blue lake. It was another beautiful day. I looked out over the sparkling water and into the distance of the green mountains on the horizon.

One more time—I died. My last words were,

"God. My money is not mine. My car is not mine. My business is not mine. Nothing is mine. It's all yours. I'm done."

I immediately felt relief. I went on,

"If you want me penniless and homeless in this day and age, I am okay with it. At least that's one thing I haven't done in my life yet. Everything is yours—including me—I'm done."

Of course, one has to absolutely mean it. Wholeheartedly. After I told my Senior Pastor about this, he let me know in no uncertain terms,

"Everything will change from this."

In 2010 and 2011, my lease went down by half from downscaling. My State Farm insurance, on their own, found a payment error and sent me a huge refund of thousands of dollars. I cashed in my GI life insurance policy I had paid into for years. I opened up my acting classes for the first time to kids. The children saved me. Home school students found my classes.

To this day, I do not have a complete explanation to give you, but in two years the $60,000 hard debt was paid off. I now have zero debt. The last three times I checked my credit score, it was 811.

Everything changed in the new life. Today, everything in my entire past life has purpose and makes sense. As I look back, there was a clear plan and a reason for everything in my life, especially the "worst parts." The most important driving force of my life was the pain.

As the end is now closer than the beginning, I very much look forward to all of the unknown and new experiences coming up around the corner. I do not want to die today—but I am ready.

I thought Act I ended when I got sober at forty-one years of age. Act II ended when I walked into the church. That was clean structure and story line. It made sense. But I was wrong again.

Two years ago, I was bleeding so much internally that it was just a question of how soon I would bleed out and die. I think this damage was from too much scotch and not eating and living right. My inside plumbing was wrecked as a price tag for hard living under pressure.

I cannot say enough praise for the Veteran's Administration hospital and health clinic. God bless the doctors, nurses, staff, and patients.

The night before I was scheduled to show up for major colon surgery at the V.A. Hospital, I began serious bleeding again. So I went into their emergency and none too soon.

The surgery went well and the most severely damaged part of my colon was removed. My spirits and feelings were high from this new lease on life. The nurses seemed surprised at the joy in my attitude and quick rebound back to health. In celebration, I opened my big mouth again,

"Thank you God! Again you have saved my life. I now know why…I will do your will for the rest of the time you have blessed me with."

The night before my early release, I went into septic shock. I guess that is what it was. I started feeling freezing cold, shaking so badly that my teeth chattered. The night nurse was a young Hispanic man who just graduated from nursing school. I scared at least five years off of his young life. In his panic, all he could say to my shaking body was his training,

"On a scale of 1 to 10. 10 being the most. What number is your level of pain?"

I yelled into his wide eyes,

"I'm not in pain!"

In panic, he started shaking and could only come up with more training,

"On a scale of 1 to 10. 10 being the most-"

"I'm freezing to death!"

The young nurse called "code" on me. Soon a platoon of scrubs filled the room, some holding suitcases. I was on the third floor of the V.A. Hospital. I.C.U. was just down the hall of the same floor. Thank God again.

In I.C.U., doctors and nurses stabilized me as about five tubes went in everywhere they could go. I spotted my dedicated V.A. surgeon showing up in the middle of the night with a worried look on his face.

This began a lesson lasting two months in the hospital. It is no secret that two months in a hospital is dangerous. I had the very best of care. The great surgical staff did everything possible. But for every step forward I took, I would get knocked two-steps back. I had an infection formed inside me the size of a fist and the consistency of putty. This deadly infection was contained but if it broke then that would be the final curtain for me. They were forced to do a risky second surgery to remove this huge infection that would not go away.

The night before this second surgery, I thanked my cherished Jewish surgeon for doing God's work with his hands. He seemed worried, so I assured him, "I've done a lot of things in my life. I wasn't shortchanged. If it's time—I'm ready."

He pulled me out of this surgery and succeeded in removing the fist-sized infection. But my plumbing was still leaking from somewhere tiny, very hard to find. I surprised myself by never once saying or even thinking,

"Why is this happening to me."

I only waivered in faith once, but recovered it back from focused reading of "the Word."

When you are laying in the hospital, sleep comes whenever you doze off. Four blood draws a day does not help. One early morning, just before the light of dawn was fully risen, I lay awake waiting for my blood draw and pulse check. By now, I had earned a window bed and was looking out at the still predawn sky. Even in a quiet time, a hospital is usually noisy. Everything grew quiet and still.

I felt and sensed a presence of a loving peace touch my left leg. I know I was not dreaming because I was waiting for the upcoming blood draw. After this touch, I did not die. From that moment on, I began to slowly get better for the first time.

The husband of my mother's caretaker worked at the V.A. Hospital. I had never met him before. He comforted me with a soothing African-American sound of speaking,

"Sometimes the Lord has to stop us. To fully get our attention."

I was previously incorrect about the beginning of Act III. It began immobilized in that bed in the V.A. Hospital. It began with my saying,

"Thank you God! Again you have saved my life. I now know why. I will do your will for the rest of the time you have blessed me with."

After losing over forty pounds and still with tubes in me, they cut me loose to recover at home (I think they were concerned about me being too long in the hospital). It took six months more to stop the infection drainage and heal up. I am now over two years downstream and have not bled again. The curtain of Act III is still risen, with this book.

My young Chinese primary care physician at the V.A. clinic put his thumb and forefinger close together and advised me,

"You came this close—a number of times."

Chinese doctors aren't prone to exaggeration. I shot back at him,

"No one told me that."

He shook his head making a squinting face,

"That would have been bad bedside manner."

"Well, we can't have that."

"Doctors are taught from internship to "drape the crepe" for the family. But you must always leave hope for the patient."

Hope is a key to faith.

The two words that made me most uncomfortable in the beginning were "God" and "Love." Now those two words are one and the same. They are now the two most important words in my life and have completely filled the empty hole that was inside me. I say unto you, I hope this helps you.

P.S. I wish to add to this chapter something that just happened to me.

Two days ago, before I began to write the first words of this chapter, I prayed as usual, for the Holy Spirit to write this chapter, even more so than the other chapters. I opened my bible to where I was in daily reading. I was in the book of Acts, Chapter 1. I lay on the couch and read the first four chapters of Acts. After finishing, I lay for a quiet moment to let the reading sink in. I was not praying and certainly had no intention of talking to myself.

I just relaxed. Then, my mouth started moving on it's own. I had no intention of speaking. Unknown sounds formed, as words in verse type structure began to flow freely from my mouth. I realized that I was speaking in unfamiliar phrases. The lilt was foreign sounding and flowed out smoothly like water. I was quite aware of speaking in this manner for about a half dozen verses. The lilt swung up and extended at the end.

This is the first time that has happened to me. I had no intention of this happening and I had no intention of writing about this. It just happened.

I tell you the truth.

If an Actor, a Spy, a Private Eye can do it—so can you.

44442053R10117

Made in the USA
Middletown, DE
07 May 2019